THE BUTTON SAMPLER

1. *Coup de Bouton*. A cartoon from 1777 in which a fashionable gentleman dazzles a lady with the brilliance of his large steel buttons.

THE
BUTTON SAMPLER

BY

LILLIAN SMITH ALBERT

AND

JANE FORD ADAMS

GRAMERCY PUBLISHING COMPANY

NEW YORK

CONTENTS

OTHER BOOKS BY

LILLIAN SMITH ALBERT

A BUTTON COLLECTOR'S JOURNAL

A BUTTON COLLECTOR'S SECOND JOURNAL

THE COMPLETE BUTTON BOOK

(with Kathryn Kent)

FOREWORD

Buttons? Why should anyone collect buttons?

To judge from the experience of a museum that has a sizeable collection, buttons still remain unconsidered trifles in the minds of many who have not yet discovered the variety and fascination of these indispensables. But visitors to the museum come, see and are conquered; and the same captivation is in store for the readers of the present book.

Both Mrs. Albert and Mrs. Adams have in the past made great contributions to the study of button history, casting light into obscure corners and charting territory previously unexplored. The present volume, summarizing with unbelievable skill the knowledge gained through a dozen years of investigation, should be of great value to beginner and old hand alike. It is certain, also, to explain why button-collecting has asserted in recent years a steadily increasing appeal, and even to make for the pastime many new devotees.

Indeed, the ladies have done their work so well in this admirable manual that it might more suitably bear another name taken from their lexicon: *The Charm String!*

CALVIN S. HATHAWAY

The Cooper Union Museum, New York

PREFACE

Every button pictured in the *Button Sampler* (excepting only the prehistoric bone one and the gold buttons from the Schliemann excavations), was chosen indvidually from examples at hand. The basis of selection in all cases was the extent to which a particular button illustrates graphically a material, technique, purpose, or other point. Without the assistance of many generous collectors who offered superior examples for photographing much would be lacking in our presentation.

For the pictorial part of the book we are especially grateful to all who put their collections at our disposal. For the text, we wish to acknowledge our indebtedness to a large button community; to librarians and museum curators who have given freely of their time and knowledge; to writers of books and articles: to students who have made unpublished findings available to us; to many in the trade who have been helpful, manufacturers, importers, and distributors of buttons; to collectors and dealers who are constantly bringing their new acquisitions to our attention; and, not the least of all, to those enthusiastic members of the National Button Society who, by their frequent inquiries to the *Button Bulletin,* encourage us to keep at work.

LILLIAN SMITH ALBERT
JANE FORD ADAMS

THE BUTTON SAMPLER

I. BUTTON LORE AND POSSIBILITIES

Buttons are among the oldest of all costume appendages. They are of infinite variety. The usual range in size is from three-eighths of an inch to about three inches in diameter. Buttons as small as one-eighth inch, as large as six inches, have been worn. They have been made of every possible material, from stone to butterfly wings, from diamonds to sawdust, from bronze to lucite.

In dating buttons we must remember that certain types were worn for centuries and others for only a season or two; that some were worn in one part of the world at one time, and in another part at another time; that some had a single vogue while others enjoyed repeated revivals. In this book we indicate only the period in which each type was popular in metropolitan centers.

Buttons have long been used in every quarter of the globe, and still are, to fasten clothing, to decorate garments, to indicate rank or position. Primitive peoples wore them to ward off evil, used them as money, and probably put them to other odd purposes as well.

2. *Prehistoric buttons.* The carved jade button (1.) was excavated at Tepe Giyan, a west Persia site, by the German archaeological expedition under Ernst Herzfeld. Dr. Herzfeld believes that it was used as a garment fastener about 4000 B.C. The gold buttons (2.) were excavated during Henry Schliemann's pioneer work at Mycenae in Greece. Some are heavy gold and shaped like studs. Others are thin sheets of gold over bone molds. Present-day research places them at about 1600 B.C.

No wonder that the collecting of them is so appealing to us or that museums today find them important for the light they throw on times past. Every woman who has saved the buttons from a dress or coat, not so much for re-use as because they were too pretty to throw away, is a button collector at heart. Every man who has brought home among his mementoes of a war a few buttons worn by soldiers of other countries, has the beginnings of a collection. The family that cherishes certain buttons for their personal associations also has the nucleus of a collection.

Fifty or sixty years ago, when nothing was thrown away lightly, buttons were carefully hoarded. Older people still remember, as one of the pleasures of going to Grandma's, the fun of opening the button box and playing with the contents. Lucky descendants who have kept Grandma's button box from the last century

3. *Tradesmen in the City of London, 1647.* A caricature broadside of the time preserved in the British Museum. Note the very great number of buttons worn.

will doubtless find in it now many buttons that amount to trash, but perhaps also a welcome number of collectibles, and even an occasional prize of outstanding interest. Before the accumulation can become a collection, the good must be separated from the bad and the best given the care it deserves.

If you are looking into the possibilities of button collecting for the first time, you will find much to intrigue you as you go along. It may be you will want to linger over the carved "pearls," or that you will wish to know the enamels by name. You may decide to buy a few picture buttons or to invest in some "paperweights." Once you have become a confirmed collector, you will keep your eyes open for buttons wherever you go, looking for such prizes as "GW's" and "ivory miniatures."

BUTTONS WITH SECRETS

The more you know about what you are looking for, the more likely you are to find it. If you know enough, you may even uncover rarities in caches where they have been overlooked by those who explored them before you. Some highly desirable buttons have eluded seasoned collectors because they were especially designed to be overlooked. Since a plain button can be worn constantly without getting any attention, the hollow

4

inside can easily serve as a secret compartment. And a fancy button can use its obvious charms to conceal a hidden intent.

During the Civil War, we are told, soldiers carried gold pieces inside their uniform buttons so that they could offer ransom, if they were captured. During World War I, our soldiers could buy buttons which met army regulations in appearance. Each one, however, in addition to its function as coat fastener was a perfect locket which could be opened and fitted with two pictures. (Plate 4.)

Not every one put such secret compartments to innocent use. Japanese artists have made for special purposes a carved ivory button in two parts with a top and bottom that screw together. The joining is concealed completely in the carving—but not for art alone. The owner who wishes may carry opium or other contraband inside the seemingly solid button.

Hiding something inside a button is kindergarten work compared to the mechanics that went into designing a camouflage compass button, such as was used in World War II. Few G.I.'s ever heard of compass buttons, for their existence was a closely guarded secret. They looked just like ordinary buttons and even under close scrutiny gave no telltale evidence of their purpose. They were issued sparingly to flyers and paratroopers of certain American and British

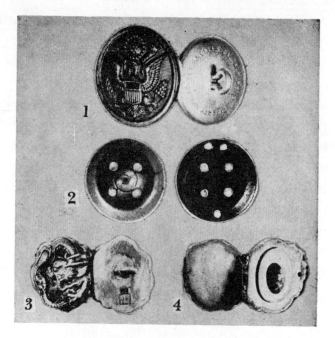

4. *Camouflaged buttons.* (1.) Locket button of World War I, opened. (2.) Compass button, in two parts, issued in World War II. Japanned magnetized steel button on right is placed on center needle of brass button on left. Two white dots at top indicate north. (3.) Silver button, front and back view. (4.) Inside of No. 3, showing hollow compartment.

commands who might be caught behind enemy lines. With the proper know-how, it was a simple matter to set up one of the buttons as a compass.

6

Buttons have been used in many other strange ways. Yet when one searches for remarkable employments and bizarre purposes, it is hard to find any greater absurdities than those dictated by Dame Fashion. The tyranny of style led gallants of the eighteenth-century French court to become walking picture galleries. They rivaled each other in the number of buttons worn, and in the audacity of the subject matter, going so far as to wear sets depicting the *Loves of Aretino,* accurately drawn to the last licentious detail. Ladies dared not look!

A similar impulse not to be outdone led others of more sedate taste to spend fortunes for buttons set with diamonds and other precious gems. At the Traphagen School of Fashion in New York City, you may see buttons "fit for a king." The king for whom they were made was Ludwig II, known to history as the Mad King of Bavaria. His passion for imitating Louis XIV is reflected in his court dress, made of cloth of gold, velvet, lace, and seed pearls. It has nearly a hundred buttons, eighty-one of them large enough to hold an incrustation of eighty seed pearls. (Plate 5.)

But button excesses have not been confined to the great and near-great. Time was, a little less than a hundred years ago, when *Godey's Lady's Book* recommended to its readers an Andalusian

7

5. *Court costume made for Ludwig II, King of Bavaria, 1864–1886.* Courtesy of Traphagen School of Fashion.

jacket trimmed with several hundred buttons. Perusal of fashion magazines will provide plenty of other examples.

Nor have button eccentricities vanished into a half-forgotten past. Quite recently a leading manufacturer distributed a booklet showing novel uses for his creations, as bracelets, earrings, and pendants made from buttons; rain hoods, leggings and scarfs fastened with them; earmuffs and umbrellas trimmed with them. There seems no more end to button uses than to button types.

DATES AND VALUES

The dating of buttons is a matter of present study. Since button collecting, as an organized hobby, goes back only to 1938, much research remains to be done. In this book, we have not attempted to do more than indicate centuries, and occasionally suggest dates in accordance with certain present-day knowledge.

We are often questioned about values. For buttons, there is nothing comparable to Scott's *Stamp Catalogue* of values for stamps, and prices of buttons today are mostly a matter of personal transaction. There are, however, several books that offer appraisals.

A warning about fakes, reproductions, and sharp practices is necessary in any discussion of button collecting, but what field of collecting has ever come of age without having to sound warnings? You must always realize that there *are* pitfalls, know where they exist, and learn to avoid them. There is no surer way of falling into them than by not knowing about them.

Unfortunately no sure rules can be given for telling a genuine old button. It is not that simple, but a matter of knowledge. You must learn. The problem is just about the same as for the collector of glass, silver, stamps, or any thing else. Painstaking study, thorough museum acquaintance with authentic buttons, exchange of ideas and experiences with other collectors, and the discrimination, which comes only through experience, are all involved in the development of button-collecting wisdom.

BUTTONS FOR YOU

Your own taste, interest, and perhaps opportunity will indicate the line of your own collecting. In this Sampler you will be introduced to every important collectible type, generally available or rare. You will find that you can assemble buttons "by subject" as in flower, portrait, or animal categories; "by materials," as metal, ceramic, ivory or pearl; or even "by use," as military. Which now shall it be? It will be a pleasure to find the fascinating answer.

II. BUTTON TYPES

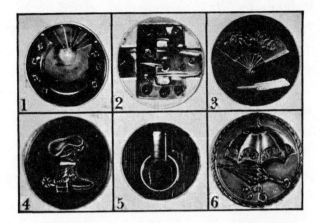

6. *Inanimate objects.* (1.) Horseshoe on a button of natural horn, studded with steel nails. (2.) Buckle carved on pearl. (3.) Fan outlined in gold on papier-mâché. These three are among the most popular inanimate subjects. (4.) Boot, plastic horn. (5.) Door knocker, vegetable ivory, movable part. (6.) Umbrella, brass. These three are uncommon. All probably made after 1875.

FLOWER BUTTONS

Button designers in many countries, using varied materials and tools, through the centuries have drawn inspiration from flowers. No wonder that it is as easy to acquire a handful of flower buttons from an antique dealer as to get a bouquet from a florist, though one must search for exact wants. Such treasures as signed Meissen buttons, with the crossed-swords mark of the famous Meissen factory, seldom go into showcases. It takes patience to locate an exquisite carved "pearl," an enamel of Limoges quality, a beautiful button of hand-wrought silver, or fine needlework, to mention a few of the types. Shirtwaist studs of hand-painted china or attractive enamels popular early in the century, are more easily found. Most plentiful of all are Victorian metal buttons, with favorites from the old-fashioned garden—roses, daisies, geraniums, pansies, forget-me-nots, violets, poppies, and other flowers.

7. (Opposite) *A bouquet of floral buttons*. (1.) Lily-of-the-valley. Carved ivory. (2.) Dresden bouquet. Porcelain with Meissen mark of crossed swords. (3.) Flower spray. Bone, painted and gilded. (4.) Geranium. Polychrome embroidery. Eighteenth century. (5.) Garden pink. Crystal with intaglio painting on back. Set in gold frame. (6.) Pansy. Reverse painting on glass. Metal frame. From France. (7.) Iris. Etched metal with color rubbed in as in damascening. Oriental work. (8.) Wild rose. Plastic horn in metal rim. British registry mark on back dates it, August 14, 1849. (9.) Chrysanthemum. Pearl, engraved, gilded, and jeweled. (10.) Forget-me-not. Chased aluminum. Made by the Scovill Mfg. Co. of Connecticut about 1890. (11.) Poppy. Hallmarked silver. Made in Birmingham, England, 1903–4. Maker J.G. 12. Rose, thistle, and shamrock, national flowers of England, Scotland, and Ireland. Gilt. (Nos. 4, 6, 8, reduced; others actual size.)

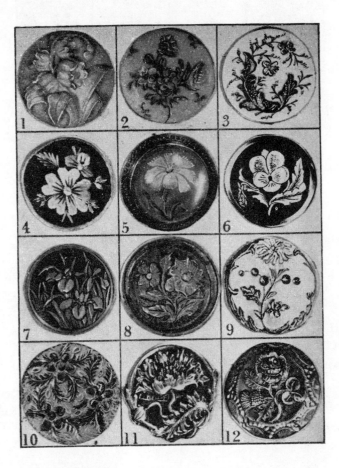

With so many flower buttons to choose from, the extra care that goes into discriminating selection, is well worth while, even beyond expectation. As a type for specialization, these have the added advantage of comparatively modest prices.

8. *Small metal buttons from about 1875.* (1.)
Grapes. (2.) Maple Leaf. (3.) Wheat. (4.) Acorn.

FRUITS, LEAVES, GRAINS, AND NUTS

Fruits, leaves, grains, and nuts follow flowers
in about that order of availability. You can find
plenty of grapes, cherries, strawberries, black-
berries, and possibly enough plums and pears,
to gather a nice showing of each kind.

Single leaves, reproduced with much fidelity,
appealed to Victorian taste. Buttons showing
ferns, grasses, and grains, especially wheat and
corn, were worn. The oak tree, its leaf and
acorn, have been cherished on buttons for centuries. Mary Queen of Scots wore jet and pearl
acorn buttons to her death.

ANIMAL, BIRD, AND INSECT BUTTONS

Plates 9, 10, and 11 were selected to illustrate
the effective use that has been made of subjects
from the animal kingdom. One can collect a favorite kind of animal and will have little trouble
finding dogs, horses, or deer. Cats, elephants,
squirrels, and others are challenges. Varied ma-

14

terials make such a grouping diversified.

PICTURE BUTTONS

When collectors speak of "picture buttons," they usually have in mind a special kind of design and also certain physical characteristics. The design is, of course, pictorial. The material is brass, white metal, or other alloy. When thick metal is used, the picture is die-struck; when thin metal, it is embossed by stamping.

In its simplest construction a button is made by soldering a shank to the back of a metal disk. The degree of elaboration that sometimes goes into construction is illustrated by the button on Plate 12. It has a balloon design, highly embossed on thin brass, fastened with cut-steel rivets to a background of pearl, the whole being set in a polished steel frame. Such buttons came into vogue in the late 1860s. They reached peak popularity during the '80s and continued in intermittent favor into this century.

Some of the pictures on old buttons are being copied on couturier buttons today. Picture buttons were worn by women and children on both indoor and outdoor garments. The considerable quantity of these buttons that have been handed down to us and, even more, the variety of pictures which we find on them, indicate the place they held in popular esteem.

Appeal of Picture Buttons

Not many years ago, nineteenth-century picture buttons were the most eagerly sought after of all types and the majority of collectors prized them above all others. Although some of their

9. (Opposite) *Animal subjects.* (1.) Cat, polychrome enamel. (2.) Cow, silver. (3.) Stag, gold inlaid in steel. (4.) Dog, carved bone set in metal frame. (5.) Elephant, tinted metal. (6.) Frog, metal set with rhinestones. (7.) Horse, silvered metal. (8.) Lamb, mosaic in gold frame. (9.) Lion, stamped brass. (10.) Monkey, carved ivory. (11.) Snake, tinted metal. (12.) Squirrel, metal. (On the whole, these were probably made in the late 1800s. No. 3, one of a set of sixteen buttons depicting the cycle of a deer, was made about 1850.)

glamor has been dimmed by a growing appreciation of the almost unlimited possibilities offered by other subjects, other materials, and other periods, picture buttons are still the favorites of many seasoned collectors.

Every well-rounded collection must have examples to represent the type. A specialized collection of picture buttons alone can include several thousand.

12. *A picture button of elaborate construction.*

Wherein lies their appeal? The answer would seem to be subject matter, the sentiment and human interest that lies in a romantic story, person, or scene. Pictures based on the simple stories

18

10. (Opposite) *Bird subjects.* (1.) Herons, painted ivory. (2.) Parrot, polychrome painting on ceramic. (3.) Hens, polychrome enamel. (4.) Swallow, woven cloth. (5.) Peacock, ivory sepia. (6.) Owl, tinted metal. (7.) Swan, soft white metal. (8.) Heron, horn inlaid with metal and pearl. (9.) Humming bird, papier-mâché in color. (10.) Eagle, pierced white metal. (11.) Rooster, stamped silver. (12.) Woodpeckers, tinted metal, a picture-button type of construction. (All are nineteenth- and twentieth-century examples, except No. 5, which is eighteenth. Nos. 3, 4, 5, 11 are actual size; others are reduced.)

of childhood, as many of them are, have pleasant associations. Little Red Riding Hood meets the wolf on several different buttons. In different poses the fox looks longingly at the grapes. Familiar Biblical characters appear, as Rebecca at the well and Moses in his cradle in the bullrushes.

Greek and Roman Inspiration

Greek and Roman myths inspired designers to picture on buttons, Jupiter with his thunderbolt, Triton blowing his trumpet, Medusa with snakes in her hair, and Cupid up to his antics. History was the inspiration for buttons picturing the landing of Columbus, Admiral Peary at the North Pole, and a whole portrait gallery of famous people. Literature, opera, and drama are

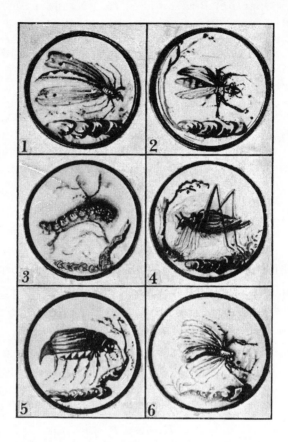

11. Realistic insect designs. Part of a set. Reverse paintings on glass drawn by an eighteenth-century artist. (One and one-half inches.)

illustrated in buttons like Don Quixote tilting at windmills, Lohengrin arriving on the swan, Maude Adams in her chanticleer costume.

13. *Story and fable buttons popular during the late nineteenth century.* (1.) Fox and Stork. (2.) Wolf and Crane. (3.) Fox and Crow. (4.) The Little Fisherman. (5.) Hop-o-My-Thumb. (6.) Red Riding Hood and Wolf. (7.) Pied Piper. (8.) William Tell and Son. (9.) Robinson Crusoe. (All specimens are found in various sizes.)

As these examples indicate, picture buttons fall naturally into classes. Some are best grouped broadly as: astronomical, mythological, oriental, religious, marine, or musical subjects. Others find their places with: buildings and scenes,

14. (Opposite) *Diversified subjects on metal picture buttons.* (1.) Saturn. (2.) Cupid Sharpening His Dart. (3.) Peary coat button. (4.) Automobiling. (5.) Incroyable and Merveilleuse. (6.) Caravel. (7.) Piano-Playing. (8.) Bellum. (9.) Billiken. (10.) Roller-Skating. (11.) Madonna and Child. (12.) Lohengrin's Arrival on the Swan. (Various sizes.)

means of transportation, pastimes and sports, theater and opera, heads and figures, babies and children, incroyables and merveilleuses (from the French, unbelievable and marvelous), cupids, gnomes, cherubs, and fairies. These constitute the types available in sufficient variety to make a good display.

Identification by Names

It is easy to identify most picture buttons with individual names. Beyond a doubt the *names* have contributed to interest and drawn attention to certain types. Some titles in use, like the jester known as Rigoletto, have been given as a matter of convenience, and for want of better identification. Others like St. George and the Dragon are accurate.

A number of identifications have been established by tracing back the picture on the button to its origin in a work of graphic or plastic art. The Sistine Madonna button is recognized at

once as coming from Raphael's painting. The
Lion of Lucerne is a realistic copy of the famous
monument. Devotees of Kate Greenaway's children (Plate 15.) are quick to see them on buttons
and to call them by name. The big dog and the

23

little dog, which Edwin Landseer called *Dignity and Impudence* when he painted them, have button counterparts. New discoveries of identifications are always being made.

From a collector's point of view the picture is the most important thing about a picture button. The next most important thing is size. General practice was to make up a picture button in three or four sizes. Pierrot and Pierrette, for instance, appear in four sizes from five-eighths of an inch to two inches in diameter. The small ones were made in much larger quantities than the large ones; the large ones are much more showy, with the result that they are at a heavy premium. When the subject is identical, the large button invariably brings a higher price than the small one; usually several times as much, in a few cases many times as much.

24

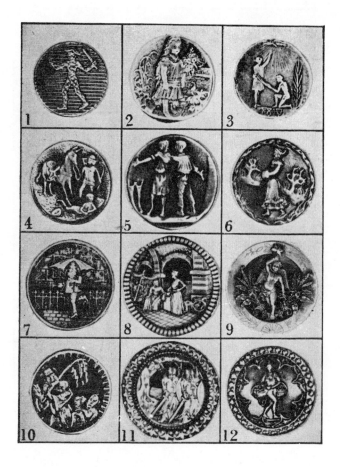

16. *Metal picture buttons not yet identified.*

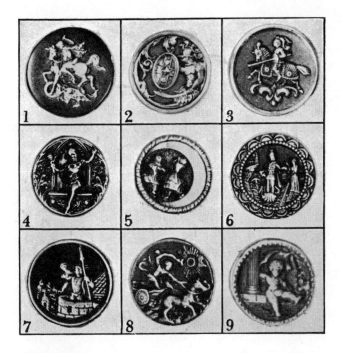

17. *Plentiful Picture buttons.* (1.) St. George and the Dragon. (2.) Aeneas. (3.) Don Quixote. (4.) Rigoletto. (5.) Pierrot and Pierrette. (6.) Lohengrin's Farewell. (7.) Sentinel at Cracow. (8.) Phaeton. (9.) Cupid at the Column. (These are probably late nineteenth century. They were made in various sizes.)

18. (Opposite) *Portrait heads from many countries*. The designers have identified them for us. (1.) Guillaume Tell. Sheffield plate. (2.) Jeanne d'Arc. Painted enamel miniature. (3.) King Charles I and Queen Henrietta. Silver. (4.) Rembrandt. Silver. (5.) Pierre Chaumette, patriot of the French Revolution. Engraving, mounted under glass. (6.) William Pitt, the Elder. Probably, like No. 5, a political button contemporary with the subject. Bronze. (7.) Napoleon. Same type, age, and material as No. 9 below. (8.) Thomas Jefferson. Made by R. Martin of Philadelphia about 1800. Sheffield plate. (9.) General Lafayette. Made in France during the General's lifetime. Brass, one piece. (10.) Abraham Lincoln. Possibly a mourning button made at the time of his death in 1865. Horn. (11.) Queen Victoria. Circulated during her Jubilee in 1887. Silvered metal. (12.) Henry W. Longfellow. Commemorating his death in 1882. Brass.

19. (Opposite) *Portrait heads of various materials.*
(1.) Stamped silver. Jacques Necker. France 1790. (2.)
Portrait of ambassador, painted on ivory, framed
under glass. (3.) Miniature, painted on ivory.
Signed by artist, AK. Probably eighteenth century.
(4.) Engraving under glass. c. 1815. (5.) Enamel
painting. Jeanne d'Arc. Nineteenth century. (6.)
Watch crystal. Sepia transfer on reverse side of
glass. About 1870. (7.) Polychrome transfer on ceramic. Late nineteenth century. (8.) Glass head
molded in high relief. (9.) Molded glass base with
painted design completely covered with tiny glass
beads cemented to the surface. (10.) Janus. Tinted
metal on wood background. (11.) Repoussé metal
mythological head superimposed on embossed
horn. (12.) Tinted metal. Edward VII. c. 1901–
1910.

The nineteenth century brought chromolithographs and photographs to the button maker. (Plate 20.) Small pictures were printed by the sheet, ready for cutting and mounting in frames.

The lithographs selected were portrait heads, scenes, and flowers. A few were put under glass and set in paste rims in the manner of ivory miniatures. Most of them were covered by clear celluloid, which dates them as after 1870.

Of the photographs, only small tintype heads of pretty girls and famous people were used at first. The tintypes were made from life, from other photographs, and from painted portraits. The popularity of Civil War generals as a subject indicates the peak of the tintype period.

Thirty or forty years later hand-tinted photographs of pretty girls, animals, and sporting scenes were mounted under celluloid. Many sets were made up, each button with a different picture, for wear on men's fancy vests.

COIN BUTTONS

What other pattern book could serve a button-designer as well as a coin catalogue? Page after page of world masterpieces are there and need no change in shape or size. Greek and Roman coins show symbols, mythological beings, and

20. *Tintype buttons.* (1.) Lincoln. (2.) Washington. (3.) Grant. *Lithograph buttons.* (4.) Charlotte Corday. (5.) Shakespeare's home (6.) Count de Fersen. *Tinted Photographs.* (7.) Part of "Road to Ruin." (8.) Jenny Lind. (9.) Sporting subjects.

rulers of antiquity; modern coins bring the story down to our own day. Perennial borrowings have been made by button-designers from this rich source of inspiration.

For centuries, silversmiths and goldsmiths have made buttons in their own way, not by

21. *Buttons either made from or copied from coins.*

copying coins, but by transforming them. The coin, with the picture portrayed on it, is just the right size and shape for a button. It needs only a shank on the back. It can also be "dapt" or shaped to a slight convexity.

If the coin is considered as raw material, all or part of the design obliterated and a new pattern created, the result is no longer a coin but a button. Such a button is then classified with others made of the same material. Plate 21 shows in Nos. 1, 2, 3, 10, and 12, coins used as raw material for buttons. Nos. 4 to 9, and 11, are of buttons with designs copied from coins. These last were never coins, despite the resemblance.

METAL BUTTONS

Any button made of gold has a place in a collection. Gold has never been beyond the button-maker's reach—quite the contrary. Literally millions of dollars worth of gold buttons have been worn. They have suffered a high mortality, however, for when styles changed, gold buttons were not put away or thrown out. They were melted down.

Silver buttons have had the same fate, but to much lesser extent. Before banking was established as it is today, a man often kept his savings in silver objects, valued by weight, though in the form of useful and decorative pieces. Silver buttons were once a normal way of employing idle capital. The practice survives in Europe where

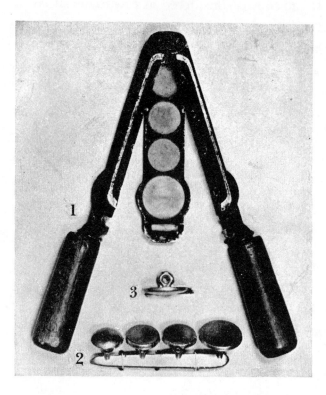

22. *Homemade button cast from pewter in a brass hand mold.* Contemporary with bullet and spoon molds. (1.) Brass mold in open position. (2.) Full casting of four buttons as they come from the mold. (3.) Finished button, cut from the bar.

peasant costumes are weighted down with silver buttons. In this country, Navaho Indians still consider their buttons as currency.

Collectors gladly accept gold buttons as they come. With silver ones they are more selective. They look for such qualities as fine craftsmanship in regional or native techniques, pleasing designs, and authentic hallmarks.

The buttons shown on Plate 23 were chosen from many collectible types.

Metals made to *look* more valuable than they are are as old as metallurgy. The most convincing way of turning the trick is to cover a base metal with a thin coating of a valuable one. In the middle of the eighteenth century, the invention of Sheffield plate, which fused a thin sheet of silver to copper, brought solid silver into competition with an excellent substitute. There was no satisfactory chemical process for silvering metal until electroplating was developed in 1838.

Gilding

The process of gilding, on the other hand, was so perfectly known that reputable eighteenth-century button-makers had to ask the English Parliament for laws to keep the unscrupulous from gilding buttons with too little gold. The approved amount would seem little

23. (Opposite) *Buttons of silver and silver plate.*
(1.) Silver "Toggle" button of the kind traditionally worn by peasants from the Baltic to the Bay
of Biscay and from Sicily to Iceland. (2.) Design
and construction typical of seventeenth- and eighteenth-century Dutch silversmithing. (3.) Silver
filigree, from Hungary, worked in the Eastern manner. (4.) Continental silver, marked 800 to indicate
the commercial grade of alloy. (5.) Sheffield plate,
silver with copper back exposed. (6.) Copper, elec-
tro-plated over the entire surface. (7.) Hand-wrought
and engraved silver caricature buttons, showing
Yankee Doodle as a macaroni. (8.) Silver with
English hallmark; Birmingham, 1902–3; Makers,
A & J Z. (9.) Niello (sulphur-silver alloy) work as
being done in Siam today. (10.) Novelty silver, now
made in Mexico. (11.) Silver in typical Navaho pattern. (12.) Silver with the American mark, Sterling.

enough, one ninety-sixth of an ounce to cover a
gross of one-inch buttons. The controversy over
the quantity of gold and the quality of the
gilding led manufacturers to stamp the backs of
buttons with claims and identification marks.
The selection of gilt buttons, shown on Plate 24,
illustrates how such marks may help collectors
in classifying and dating buttons. Another guide
to dates lies in makers' names. When a name
appears on a button-back, it can often be traced
through old directories and town histories and
the date of business established. Marks indicat-
ing quality are difficult to trace.

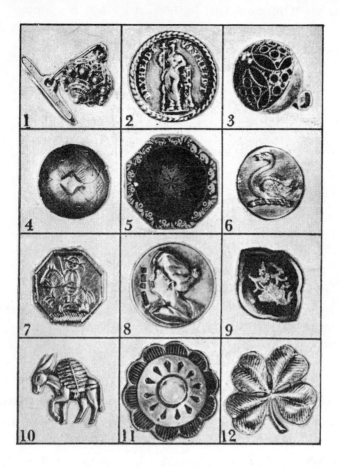

Attempts to simulate gold and silver with cleverly compounded alloys gave pinchbeck (for gold) and tombac (for silver) to eighteenth-century button-makers. In the nineteenth century, nickel alloys, such as German and Chinese "silver," got wide acceptance.

24. (Opposite) *Gilt buttons.* (1.) Plain, flat button of heavy metal, back-marked "Double Gilt" to show that twice the legal minimum of gold was applied. (2.) Similar construction. Marked for fine color. (3.) American eagle, intended for American markets. (4.) Hand-chased floral pattern, rose, shamrock, and thistle. (5.) Freehand linear design, hand-chased. (6.) Watchcase gilt. The background is watered metal, the ornament is highly embossed. (7.) Die-struck floral pattern of fine workmanship. (8.) The same pattern enhanced by hand-chasing. (9.) English. Dated by its back-mark of S. Firmin as eighteenth century. (10.) American. Dated by its back-mark as made between 1836 and 1844. (11.) A. P. & Cie., the back-mark of Albert Parent & Company of Paris. (12.) Thin metal, hollow construction with tin back. The final stage of the gilt button. (All nineteenth century except No. 9.)

Pewter and "Hard White"

Pewter, a tin alloy, was the poor man's button metal for centuries. Sometimes it mimicked silver, and sometimes it developed its own individuality. In England, the quality of the alloy suitable for button-making was set up by law in 1615. In America, a distinctive alloy was developed about 1820. It was called "hard white," and buttons were so stamped. Being a unified group of similar patterns and identical construction, hard-white buttons make an interesting speciality for the collector. Late in the

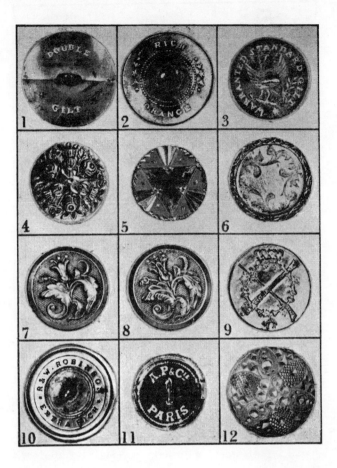

century a heavily-leaded alloy had a vogue. Britannia metal, the most diversified of the tin alloys, can be compounded to resemble either silver or gold.

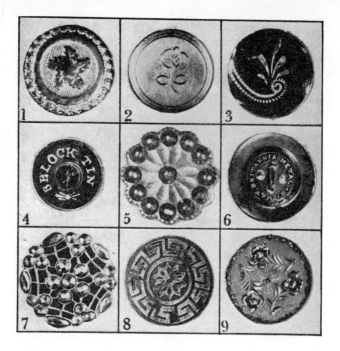

25. *Metal buttons of many types.* (1.) American pewter, marked Hard White. (2.) Fine pewter. (3.) White metal, lacquered and bright-cut. (4.) Pure tin. (5.) Eighteenth-century steel. (6.) Britannia metal. (7.) Nineteenth century, stamped steel facets (8.) Flat steel, stamped. (9.) Hand-chased aluminum.

Block Tin

That block tin had at least a recognized use is proven by the existence of buttons with the back-mark, "block tin." (Plate 25.) Tin plate, similar to tin-can metal, was used for button fronts. Tinned backs are characteristic of many picture buttons as well as other two-piece constructions after 1870.

Brass

Of all metals and alloys, brass is the one that has been most used in buttons. It would doubtless be safe to say that more buttons have been made from brass than from all other metals put together. The advantages of brass, aside from availability, are that it makes a good appearance; it is ductile and malleable; it is strong and durable; it can be worked hot or cold, with hand tools or heavy machinery; it can be molded, hammered, stamped, chased, etched, or engraved; it can be gilded, plated, or enameled; it combines well with other materials.

Brass buttons are so infinite in their variety that it would be impossible to catalogue them all. The collector's favorites among them are the gilts, the uniforms and a kind called "Colonials." These last are a classic type worn in Europe and America from the seventeenth century until well into the nineteenth. Early collectors gave the name to certain buttons handed down in this country from colonial times.

Colonials are one-piece, handmade, metal buttons (not always of brass, though usually so),

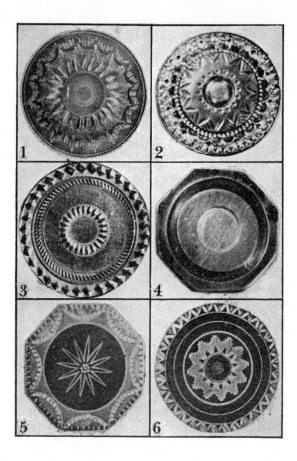

26. *Metal "Colonial" buttons.* All except No. 4 hand-chased or engine-turned. Actual size.

with hand-drawn metal wire shanks lightly brazed on. Chasing tools and punches played an important part in their ornamentation. Plate 26 gives a general idea of their appearance. You must see and handle them to become familiar with their characteristics.

Copper has been used in the same ways as brass but to a much more limited extent. Bronze, which resembles copper, has had restricted use in buttons.

Steel

Steel made a spectacular appearance as a button material in the mid-eighteenth century when it emerged as a luxury metal, competing on equal terms with gold and silver. As much skill and expense was then lavished upon the cutting, polishing, and setting of steel facets as upon a gem. The facets, hand-cut and hand-polished, were riveted to solid bases of highly-polished metal where they sparkled like diamonds in the candlelight.

In a nineteenth-century revival of cut steel the facets were riveted to filigree frames, giving a lacy effect. When the lowest-price market demanded cut steel, a number of economies were made. In 1890, the complete button was made from thin sheet metal stamped into facets, thus eliminating cutting and riveting. In the nineteenth century, solid steel buttons ran more to tinted, engraved, stamped, gilded, and painted designs than to simple brilliance, as seen in the earlier century.

Aluminum is the last metal (though new *alloys* appear constantly), introduced to button-making. The first aluminum buttons known to us were shown in London in 1862. At that time, pure aluminum was still expensive and, as long as it remained scarce, only ornamental buttons were made of it. Utility buttons of aluminum began to appear in the early 1900s, when the metal went into mass production. For some reason, aluminum has still to establish itself as a widely used material for either fancy or common buttons. To this day an aluminum button is almost a curiosity.

MILITARY BUTTONS

In the history of buttons, the military type put in a comparatively late appearance. The development of a particular style with special designs intended for wear only on military uniforms belongs to the eighteenth century. Until about 1750, it had been customary for fighting forces to wear the same kind of buttons as civilians and to choose any pattern.

The trend toward specialization crystallized between 1760 and 1770. In that decade both the English and French armies authorized the placing of regimental numbers or corps emblems on

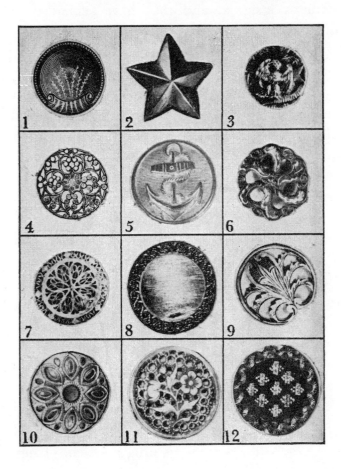

27. *Nineteenth-century dress buttons.* Stamped, pierced, filigreed, engraved, or chased brass.

their buttons. The innovation was so popular that by the end of the century, buttons had become established as an essential part of the soldier's insignia, and they have remained so until today.

As the nineteenth century advanced, armies and navies in every part of the world took pride in splendid buttons. Even an upstart in a tiny kingdom, Henri Christophe of Haiti, provided his troops with imported buttons of the best quality.

The French lavished such meticulous care on design and execution that their military buttons were comparable to their coins. Louis Fallou, an authority in the field, demonstrated how many *kinds* of buttons the French have had by identifying 3700 (mostly military), worn between 1762 and 1914.

As thorough a compilation of British buttons would be at least as long. The British custom has been to give each regiment a button of its own. From a simple beginning of a regiment wearing its number, there has evolved an array of emblems, cyphers, mottoes, battle honors, and other designations rivaling a system of heraldry. Consider, for example, the significance of the button worn by the 55th Regiment between 1855 and 1881. In the center is a battle honor, symbolized by the Dragon of China; at the top is a loyalty emblem, the Victorian crown; at the bottom is the regimental number, 55; and around the edge is the laurel wreath for victory.

The number of different American buttons, strictly military in nature (even including those of the Republic of Texas and the Confederacy), is quite small. Judging from the few hundred needed, you might expect to get a complete collection. Yet the feat has not yet been accomplished by any single person though some have worked on it for years.

Around the turn of the century a handful of men saw the importance of military buttons here. Under the auspices of the New-York Historical Society they carried on systematic excavations of the camp sites of the Revolution and also of Indian burial grounds. To the buttons thus literally unearthed, they added others, uncovered through diligent search and persistent inquiry of which collectors are masters.

Choosing the name, American Buttonist Society, they founded the first button collector's club on record. By working together in the field and in the library, the members left us more than mementoes, for their findings provided historians with knowledge of troop movements during the Revolution.

Their combined resources and energies assembled several of our finest collections of military buttons. Luckily for us, much of their work is preserved in museums. One member, Luis Emilio, gave his complete collection to the

28. *Rare uniform buttons.* (1.) Continental Army. (2.) 1st Battalion Pennsylvania Continental Army. (3.) 1st Regiment Artillerists & Engineers. (4.) U.S. Infantry. (5.) 1st Regiment Light Artillery. (6.) U. S. Navy. (All six made before 1820.) (7.) Texas Navy. (8.) Voltigeurs. (9.) Confederate Army.

Essex Institute of Salem, Massachusetts. Much of the Hart collection is in the Lightner Museum at St. Augustine, Florida. The New-York Historical Society, as sponsor, always had first choice of all specimens excavated.

The quest for early and rare items becomes increasingly spirited as appreciation of them grows. A chronological arrangement of our military buttons is particularly interesting because we began fighting our battles at about the same time that soldiers began wearing distinctive buttons. Thus our military history offers a complete collection of types.

At intervals new manufacturing methods have altered the general appearance of *typical* military buttons. New designs were introduced when branches of the service were reorganized, when new governments came to power, and for other reasons as well. As military buttons became a prototype for all uniform buttons, many resembling them came into use.

NON-MILITARY UNIFORM BUTTONS

Uniform buttons of all kinds offer a challenge to the industry and imagination of the hobbyist. Even a miscellaneous assortment can be arranged into an artistic display. A group carefully selected from a single city, state, or section of the country can chart the growth of a region. A highly specialized topical collection, made up of buttons from a single industry, such as railroading, or an activity, like firefighting, can fit into your own occupation, or preoccupation.

Think for a moment of the uniform buttons

29. (Opposite) *Non-military uniform buttons from New York City.* All actual size. (1.) Department of Docks. (2.) Health Officers' Department. (3.) Yacht Club. (4.) New York and Brooklyn Bridge. (5.) The Barclay Hotel. (6.) Grand Central Depot. (7.) Brooklyn Rapid Transit. (8.) Interborough Rapid Transit Company. (9.) Third Avenue Railroad. (10.) Fire Department. (11.) New York Hospital. (12.) Municipal Police.

you see from day to day. Notice them on the postman, the fireman, the policeman, the street-carman, the usher in the theater, the elevator operator in the public building, the staff in the hotel lobby, the schoolboy from a private acad-emy—the list could go on and on.

Buttons made for occupational and ceremonial uniforms far outnumber the military in this country, and no wonder. Government depart-ments with no military authority value an im-pressive uniform for the respect it evokes. Certain lines of business and industry, notably transpor-tation lines, regard a uniformed staff as an essen-tial evidence of prestige. Numerous patriotic and fraternal organizations prefer a uniform to any other style of ceremonial dress for their bands and other marching units.

The uniform, with its special buttons serving as identification, gives the wearer recognized position. Uniforms are worn in some cases to

show that the wearer belongs in a select circle, that he is a member of an aristocratic club; on the other hand the uniform may mark the wearer as a menial. In France, the hunt-club button is a symbol of snobbery. Members of such clubs are

30. *Sporting and Hunt Clubs.* (1-3.) Scovill Manufacturing Co., Waterbury, Conn., about 1840. (4-6.) Worn by titled persons in France. (4.) Berry Solone —Vte. de Montsaulnen. (5.) Vicomte de Fadata. (6.) Marquis de la Roche. (7-9.) Highly gilded, engraved one-piece hunt-club buttons. England. (7.) Elkridge Hounds. (8.) N. Buckinghamshire Harriers. (9.) Groton.

called "boutons," that is, persons entitled to wear the official club buttons. Livery and crest buttons (Plate 31.), mark the wearers as belonging to the service of a titled or influential household.

Hunt-club, sporting, livery, crest, and monogram buttons are among the finest example of design and metalwork. They are attractive both for their beauty and their associations. Having their beginnings in the eighteenth century, they were most widely used in the mid-nineteenth, and are now almost obsolete.

QUASI-UNIFORM BUTTONS

There are buttons which might be called quasi-uniform, for they look like uniform buttons though there are no uniforms to which they belong. Buttons of the Grand Army of the Republic are examples. The Army always had buttons but never uniforms. The thousands of Civil War veterans who marched in parades wore their regular suits. The usual buttons, however, were replaced by shiny brass ones marked G.A.R. Thus the buttons served almost to transform ordinary clothes into uniforms.

Brass campaign buttons are another illustration. The wearer of these proclaims his loyalties, rather than his permanent affiliation with an organization. The first campaign button worn in the United States was a small, flat, plain, brass

31. (Above) *Livery buttons showing varied crests*. Specialization may be according to finish, as silvered or gilt, or in one subject as birds, animals, inanimate objects, figures, etc. Eighteenth-century examples are generally of solid silver or Sheffield plate. Later examples are plated with gold or sil ver over copper. (Sizes range generally from ⅝ of an inch for sleeves, 1 inch for coats, to 1½ inches for cloaks or overcoats.)

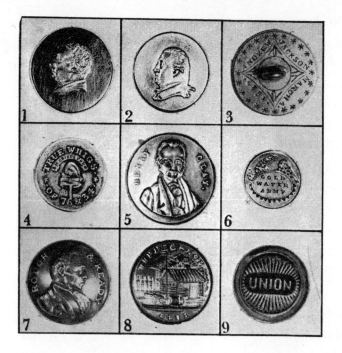

32. (1.) General Lafayette button, made to cele-
brate his 1824 visit to the U.S. (2.) Gilt restrike of
gold buttons presented to Lafayette in 1824. Nos.
3, 4, 5, 7, and 8. Campaign buttons of 1828, 1834,
1844, 1848, and 1840. (6.) Temperance button,
1840s. (9.) Patriotic button of 1860s. (The buttons
are actual size, brass, highly gilt.)

one, which hid its political message on the underside. The inscription on the *back* of the button read, "Andrew Jackson, March 4, 1829."
(Plate 32, 3.)

In 1834 the Whig Party used similar small,

flat, brass buttons, this time with a political message on both front and back. One Whig button, about the size of a dime, carries on the front two mottoes, "E Pluribus Unum" and "For the Constitution," together with a Liberty Cap on a pole. On the back, this button is marked, "True Whigs of 76 & 34." No space was wasted!

The Harrison-Tyler campaign of 1840 and the Zachary Taylor campaign of 1848 were both prolific of buttons. By that time, uniform buttons were made as they are today, with a flat back and a high rounded top. Many of the Harrison buttons featured the log cabin, with which this president was identified. The cabin's surroundings were varied to suit local taste; on some a tobacco plant, on others a flag flying, on most, a cider barrel prominently placed. The supporters of Taylor chose his portrait and the slogan, "Hero of Buena Vista."

From the political buttons, it is just a step to the non-partisan patriotic type, which display the American flag, American eagle, the Liberty Bell, or a slogan. During the Philadelphia Centennial in 1876, patriotic buttons were the rage.

Good causes have also been espoused on quasi-uniform buttons. The members of a children's temperance society of the early 1840s wore small brass buttons, neatly stamped "The Cold Water Army." An open Bible accompanied by a pious thought is seen on buttons of the same period. One button bears the cryptic message, " 'Tis Well, 8910."

PSEUDO-UNIFORM BUTTONS

Uniform buttons were used as a basis for the design of purely costume buttons. The design remains, but the function is lost. (Plate 27, 3, 5.) Button makers now produce buttons for women's and children's clothing, using designs from uniform buttons. When the material is brass and the size and shape regular, these buttons can be confusing. However, the difference between the uniform buttons and the ones meant for ordinary wear is usually quite apparent, if you examine construction and die-work. Uniform buttons must be exceptionally strong for they get long, hard wear. Costume buttons, on the other hand, are perfectly satisfactory when of light construction. The design on a costume button can be sketchy; on the official button, it must be perfect to the last detail.

GEORGE WASHINGTON INAUGURAL BUTTONS

The George Washington Inaugural buttons (often called "G.W.'s"), belong in a class by themselves. There are no others like them and no others so prized among American historical buttons. These are flat metal buttons bearing designs appropriate to Washington's inauguration as the first president. The monogram G.W., the legends, "Long Live the President," "Remember March Fourth 1789," and "Memorable ÆRA," the American eagle, a likeness of Washington, and a chain of the thirteen states were used. More than a dozen different patterns have come down to us in sizes from about half-an-inch to nearly an inch and a half in diameter. (Plate 33.)

The original owners valued them highly and wore them for years, probably as long as Washington was alive. For us they perpetuate the spirit of a memorable era, an important period. On the centenary of the inauguration, in 1889, commemorative buttons, similar in appearance though not exact copies, were struck. They too are now collector's items.

"PEARLS" AND OTHER SHELLS

Mother-of-pearl buttons, or "pearls," as they are known, owe their appeal to the natural beauty of the material; some white, some soft grey, some a golden brown, some a blending of tints—and all of iridescent radiance. The changeable play of underlying colors is equally pleasing

33. *Washington Inaugurals.* One-piece brass, actual size.

whether the button is perfectly plain or carved, dyed, or embellished with other trim.

Though we see many pearls among eighteenth-

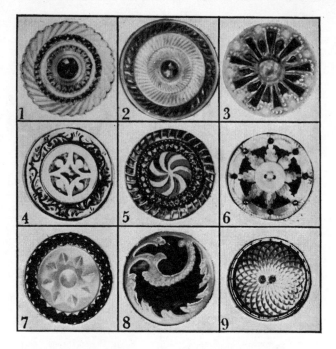

34. *Conventional pearl buttons.* Row 1, Nos. 1-3.
Eighteenth-century types with foil, paste and other
ornamentation. Nos. 4-6. Nineteenth-century types,
carved with a power tool. Nos. 7-9. Also nineteenth century. Set in metal frames.

century buttons and some earlier than that, the
large scale *trade* of pearl button making dates
from about 1825. In the years between 1825 and
1850, hundreds of small artisans worked for themselves, turning out pearl buttons with no more
equipment than a man might set up in his

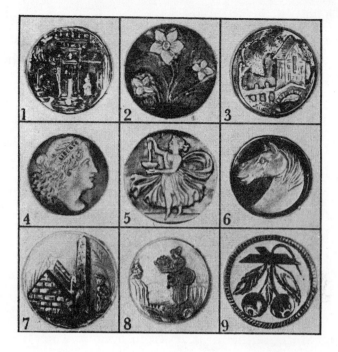

35. *Nineteenth-century cameo-carved pearl buttons.* Nos. 1-3. Abalone with gold accents in the designs. Nos. 4-6. Dark base shading to white. Nos. 7 and 8. White base shading to brown. No. 9. Dyed snail with cut steel trim. (All buttons reduced in size.)

kitchen. After 1850, power machines for cutting blanks and for carving patterns led to large-scale production. It was then that the "common pearl" became a utility article indispensable to each household.

Pearl button making required much hand

labor, even after the introduction of machines. In fact it still does. The finest pearl buttons have always required the skill of master craftsmen who place the stamp of ability upon their work.

Collectors appreciate most those pearl buttons from the eighteenth and early nineteenth centuries which, in addition to fine color and luster, have superior clear-cut, well-placed designs. Machine-made pearls are selected chiefly for quality of shell and attractiveness of pattern. For natural beauty, the shell of the abalone, native to American waters, is unsurpassed. Its light shades have fire, brilliant enough to illuminate deep-tone dyes. The dark green variety is unsurpassed in both brilliance and color.

Since mother-of-pearl from oceanic waters was considered of better color, fresh-water shells were

36. (Opposite) *Shells.* (1.) A carved cowrie shell. Paste rim. Figure and scene are brown and white, the background lavender. (2.) Volute shell, engraved and highlighted with gold pigment. (3.) A scene carved on queen's conch with pink background. Set in a paste rim. (4.) Cameo head carved on queen's conch. Elaborately set in filigreed mother-of-pearl, studded with cut steel. (5.) Cameo head carved in bull's-mouth shell, with sharp color contrasts. Steel studded, pierced metal mounting. (6.) A masterpiece of carving, which employs the full resources of cowrie shell. Ornate white metal rim.

little used for buttons. But this custom was radically changed in 1890, when an Austrian immigrant set up trade on the banks of the Mississippi and began cutting buttons from clamshells. Within ten years his venture had reached a mass-production basis that shook the old button-making centers in England, France, and Austria. After 1900 ocean pearl met severe competition.

Buttons made from shells which are not nacreous, or iridescent, are sometimes called "shells" to distinguish them from "pearls." (Plate 36.) Among the shells used for color but with no iridescence, the leading ones are the brown and white mottled *cowrie* with a lavender underlayer, the *volute* with a translucent rosy tint, the *bull's-mouth* with its dark red underlayer, and the pinkish *queen conch*. These are the same shells used by jewelers who mount cameos; the carved centers of shell buttons are exactly like the ones used in brooches and rings.

CLEAR AND COLORED-GLASS BUTTONS

Within the memory of some people, children and young ladies made a game of gathering buttons for Charm Strings. A proper string included no duplicates, and the aim was to have 999 buttons on it. Though several generations made Charm Strings, and handed them down in the family, regrettably few survive intact. The earlier ones have suffered especially from breakage, since they included more glass buttons than the later strings.

Small glass buttons, the size of the end of a finger, came and went between 1835 and 1880 in

37. Section from an early Charm String. All buttons from before 1880.

a rainbow of colors. Most of them were made in Bohemia, where women and children, supplied with glass, lamps, and hand-operated molds, carried on the work as a household industry. The

67

fine quality of the glass assured it fashion success, while low production costs in Bohemia defied extensive competition from any other country. Very few of the later colored glass buttons matched these in variety and ornamental trim. (Plate 37.)

38. (Opposite) *Types of glass buttons.* Patterns seen through a glass top. (1.) Watch crystal. A thin glass lens painted on the reverse, ornamented with pearl tesserae, attached to wide shank-plate by waxy adhesive. (2.) Paper-back. A disk of fancy paper is pasted to the flat back of a domed shape. (3.) Painted-back. Pattern-molded intaglio in the back, depressions filled with pigment. (4.) Lacy. A flat or slightly rounded button, named for lacy pattern embossed on face, highlighted by metallic paint on back. Only late-Victorian type shown. All others are Charm String glass, (5, 6.) Kaleidoscope, front and in parts. Disk of ornamental paper or foil protected by shank-plate as wide as paper. Dome-shaped tops. (7-12.) Front and side views of "reflector," "glory," and "dewdrop." A tiny spot of color at the shank diffuses color throughout. (11.) Several stripes or (12.) dots of color on back become star or medallion on face (13-20.) Paperweights. Transparent glass, applied over separately made designs. (13.) Cross-sections of glass canes. (14.) Opaque glass center, with foil stars. (15.) Foil design with faceted top. (16.) Fancy molded top over glass flower on base. (17.) Fluted top over twisted-cane base. (18.) Opaque white base with rose. (19.) Rose on latticino background, fancy molded top. (20.) Opaque white cameo head set on cranberry base. Called a sulphide paperweight, rarest of all.

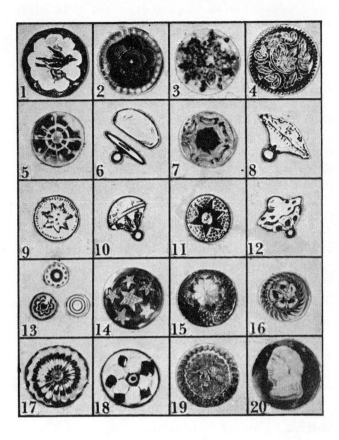

Makers of Charm Strings loved these buttons for their gay colors and their "eyes." The eyes, as the metal loop-shanks were then called, were threaded onto the string, allowing several buttons to cluster together in jewel-like array.

These buttons, so typical of older strings, are

39. (Opposite) *Glass buttons.* (1.) Clear glass, back molded in hobnail pattern. (2.) Slag, also called marble glass. (3.) Mirror. Actual looking glass on a wide shank. (4.) Opaque white, called milk glass. (5.) Back view showing swirl around loop shank. (6.) Coronet shape. Base and tip molded separately. (7.) Heart-shaped swirl. (8.) Fluted shape, with swirl back. (9.) Pin shank. Like a pin doubled, passing loosely through the button and spreading at the back. (10.) Metal-banded. Bands attached to shank. (11-15.) Overlay trim. Softened glass applied over the outside. (11.) Banded. (12.) Dotted. (13.) Spiral twist. (14.) Spatter. (15.) Flower. (16.) Overlay sheath. Glass core, covered with glass. This one is spun, or thread, glass sheath. (17.) Hollow, blown, glass ball with self-shank. (18.) Self-shank molded with the button. Side view. (19.) Victorian opaque. Sometimes called colored milk glass. (20.) Fluted shape with metal bracelet for trim.

now known as Charm String glass. They form a recognized branch of specialization and offer as absorbing a quest now as they did when Charm Strings were being made. Devotees of the type have given appropriate names to the different colors, shapes, and construction features. Colors and shapes are, for the most part, easily understood. Ruby, amber, and milk glass are among the colors. Shapes include balls, cones, cubes, stars, fluted-sides and miniature objects.

Names like swirl-back, self-shank, overlay, reflector, kaleidoscope, and paperweight indicate

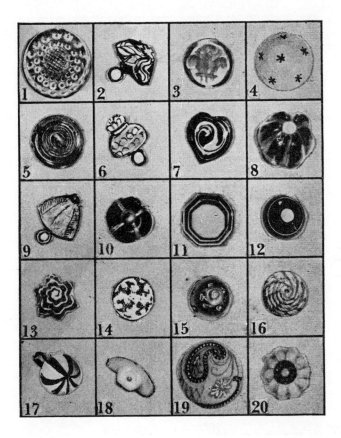

structural qualities. A swirl-back is so called from the winding off of the glass around the shank in a twist or swirl. A button with a slotted projection of the glass on the back, instead of a metal shank for carrying the thread, is called a self-shank. Sew-through, or hole buttons, are not common on Charm Strings.

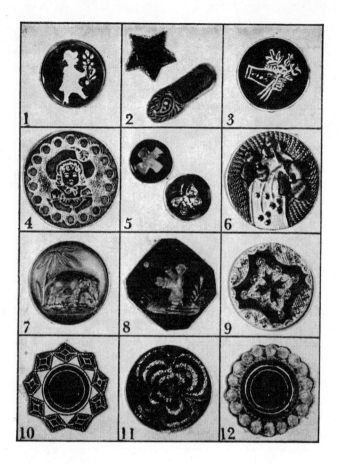

40. Black-glass, typical of last half of nineteenth century.

BLACK GLASS

Until about a hundred years ago black glass buttons differed from other glass buttons only in color, not in shape, size or pattern. Then black glass took on its own patterns, and became typed under the name "jet." That term has been troublesome, since collectors must remember that nearly every "jet" button is jet-black glass and that buttons made of real, mineral jet are rare.

To say that jets were fashionable during the last half of the nineteenth century seems almost to miss the point, for fashions come and go. Black glass buttons came and, after Queen Victoria chose them for personal wear, remained to be taken for granted as always in good taste, correct for all time.

The simple, faceted ones in solid black suited the most dignified matron or lady in mourning. Those finished in silver luster had a dazzling brilliance, as well they might since platinum was the source. Gold, silver, and iridescent lusters were elegant enough for the finest ball dress. And there were patterns for every taste, from realistic elephants to romanticised children.

"JEWEL" BUTTONS

Buttons which have a glass center and a metal rim are called "jewel," whether or not the glass is gemlike. There are three types of jewel buttons, all from the nineteenth century: Waistcoat, Victorian, and Gay-Nineties.

Waistcoat jewels are small, usually a half inch

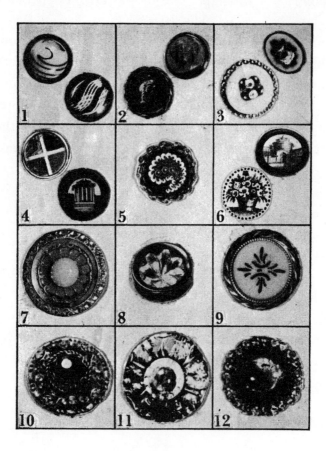

41. *"Jewels."* Nos. 1-3. Waistcoat. Nos. 4-6. Mosaic waistcoat. Nos. 7-9. Victorian. Nos. 10-12. Gay Nineties.

across. They have narrow rims. The centers may be perfectly plain, though most of them are decorated with swirls, inlays, goldstone, molded tops (including cameo heads), or in other ways.

Victorian jewels include a variety of larger buttons with simple or decorative rims and large glass centers. Black, white, and clear glass outnumber colors in this group.

Gay-Nineties jewels are the largest and fanciest of all. Many made for opera cloaks and fur wraps are quite spectacular, with ornate metal frames and large, brilliant, glass insets.

PASTE BUTTONS

Paste is glass prepared in any of the specialized ways that make it resemble precious or semiprecious stones. Diamonds, being the showiest of the precious stones, are the ones most copied. The sparkling paste that imitates them is still called "strass" for its originator, Josef Strasser, who introduced his invention about 1750. After Germany became the center of production, the name "rhinestone" meant diamond paste.

Paste gems often get their brilliance from being backed with foil or metallic paint. The colored pastes emeralds, rubies and sapphires particularly need such treatment. Among semiprecious stones, agate has been the most widely and most successfully copied in glass. Often an expert mineralogist and his tools are needed to distinguish false from true. Garnets are well copied in red glass. Green glass can be made to look quite

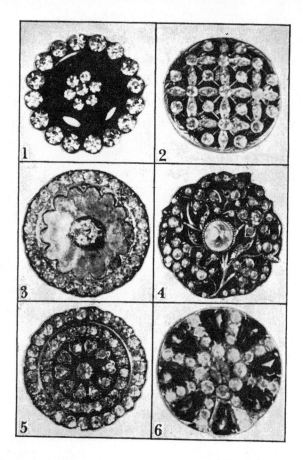

42. *Diamond and colored pastes set in silver.* Actual size. Late eighteenth and early nineteenth century.

like jade, and pink glass can readily pass for rose quartz.

Pastes are shaped in facets or cabochon and mounted in the same manner as real stones.

76

Buttons set with diamonds were once the delight of kings and princes, as is shown by the records of 1685, when Louis XIV acquired a hundred and twenty-three diamond buttons in the month of July alone. Almost no diamond-studded buttons have survived, however. A few masterpieces, like the jeweled morse button, made by Cellini for Pope Clement VII, are preserved in museums. But most of them have been broken up for the obvious reason that the diamonds were wanted.

Buttons set with semiprecious stones, on the other hand, have had exceptional survival, for when fashions changed they were carefully put away. On Plate 43 are illustrated some of the popular gems and stones and some of the characteristic mountings.

CERAMIC BUTTONS

Ceramic buttons get their varied qualities from different bodies (as the potter calls the prepared clay), from different glazes, and from different methods of ornamentation. One ceramic body produces jasper ware, another yields stone china. One glaze gives a matt finish, another brilliance. Decoration can be added by putting color di-

43. (Opposite) *Buttons set with precious and semi-precious stones.* (1.) Silver button with emeralds, rubies, and pearls. (2.) Diamonds in gold. (3.) Marcasites in silver. (4.) Seed pearls and sapphires in silver. (5.) Carnelian with marcasites in silver. (6.) Garnets in silver. (7.) (above) Coral set in gold; (below) tigereye. (8.) Four-hole jade. (9.) (above) Smoky agate; (below) Jasper. (10.) Fortification agate. (11.) Moss agate. (12.) Jet. (Nos. 1, 7, 9. In actual size; the rest reduced. Nos. 1-4. From eighteenth century; the rest, nineteenth century.)

rectly on the button (hand-painting is the usual way), by putting it on indirectly (transferred from a decalcomania), or by a combination of these methods.

The three characteristics of Satsuma buttons are a semiporcelain body, unique crackle glaze, and highly stylized decorations. Birds, flowers, butterflies, insects, and dragons, drawn in rich colors and gold with an endless elaboration of detail, remind us of Japanese prints. Persons, real and mythological, are artfully posed. Scenes are enchantingly unreal. Plate 44.

The Japanese have made these buttons for export since the 1870s, with peak output around the turn of the century. They form the largest group of commercially hand-decorated ceramic buttons we have.

Comparatively small numbers of buttons have been hand-painted commercially except in the

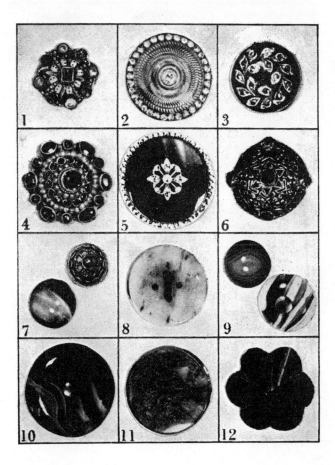

Orient, one reason being that Europeans found
a perfect way to print patterns on buttons almost
as soon as they learned the secret of making
porcelain. The process, invented in Liverpool,

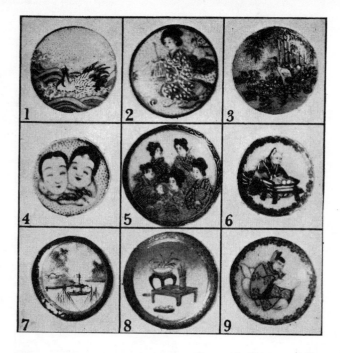

44. *Satsuma buttons.* Made in Japan for export. Various sizes.

consists of laying a transfer paper (decalcomania) on a ceramic base and firing the piece. The decalcomania is impregnated with a picture made in such a way that the entire design will separate or transfer from the paper and adhere to the new surface. A decalcomania for use in ceramics must have pigments which become glasslike when fired in a kiln. Plate 45.

45. *Nineteenth-century ceramics with transfers.* (1, 2, 4, 8, 10.) Monochrome. (3, 5, 6, 7, 9, 11, 12.) Polychrome. (3, 5, 11.) Enamel trim.

Although the actual printing is done mechanically, transfers require handwork to place the patterns evenly. Often a "decal" is used only to get an outline, all of the finishing being painted by hand. Plate 45.

The basic technique of transfers, invented in Liverpool in the eighteenth century, is still used. Its versatile possibilities permit the use of gold and silver, monochrome or polychrome. A metallic background with embellishments appears to be illuminated; a black outline looks exactly like a pen-and-ink drawing; a blending of transfer work with hand-painting can rival a painted miniature.

Transfers helped make china a practical material for low-priced buttons. During the 1830s, a new way was found for molding small porcelain objects with greater speed and less firing loss. As a whole block of blanks could be printed from one large transfer sheet, production of pretty utility buttons boomed.

"Calico" buttons, made in this way with patterns copied from calico cloth, became a fifty-year staple. More than two hundred different patterns are known. All of the common cloth colors, red, blue, green, black, brown, lavender, pink and orange, were used. Sizes ranged from less than three-sixteenths of an inch to about one and one-eighth inches.

Plain white glazed buttons were worn at the same time. Some had crimped edges, called piecrust, and some had hobnail borders. Some edges were banded with color or gold.

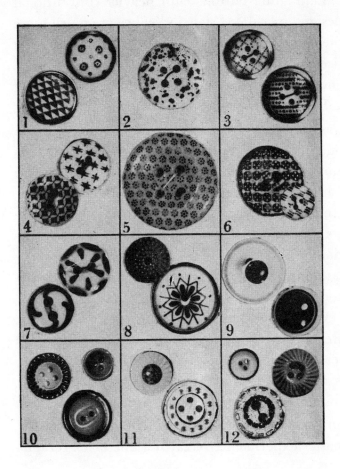

46. (Above) *Porcelain buttons for daily use.* Actual sizes. (1.) "Jewel" calico. (2.) Spatter design. (3.) Brass rims added. (4, 6.) Two- and three-hole designs in colored and white bodies. (5.) Four-hole calico design. (7.) Stencils. (8.) One-hole or whistle pattern. (9.) Self-shank and bull's-eye. (10, 12.) Two-, three-, and four-hole solid color, color-banded, luster, gold-trim, and piecrust. (11.) Piecrust with self-shank and hobnail pattern.

Late china buttons with heavier conventional designs are called "stencils." They are much more plentiful than calicoes, though found in fewer sizes, colors, and patterns. Plate 46 shows these and other types of utility porcelain buttons.

Forty or fifty years ago, when china-painting was a great accomplishment, potteries made smooth, white, porcelain buttons especially for amateur artists to decorate. Thousands of these "shirtwaist" buttons have been preserved. Some are beautifully painted and expertly fired. Others are of mediocre workmanship. Flowers, especially roses, seem to have been the favorite decoration, then monograms, and miniature heads and figures. Plate 47, Nos. 10, 11, 12.

Wedgwood buttons, like the ones on Plate 49, are usually considered the most desirable of all ceramic buttons. The reason (aside from rarity), is not hard to find. Company records, made by Josiah Wedgwood himself, attach considerable importance to button production. In 1768, the master experimenter created a fine black ceramic

47. (Opposite) *Ceramic buttons decorated without transfers.* Among rare and prized ceramic buttons are those bearing potters' marks. (1.) Copenhagen. (2.) Meissen. (3.) Sevres. (4.) Chantilly. (5.) Coalport. (6.) Ruskin. (7.) Floral design, eighteenth century. (8, 9, 10, 12.) Polychrome floral groupings, gold trim. (11.) Polychrome hand-painting.

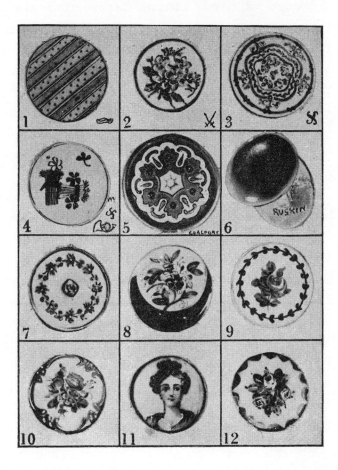

body which he named basaltes. Six years later he perfected his parian-like jasper ware. From the first, he made small medallions suitable for mounting in button frames of silver, copper, steel, pearl or other materials. After 1786, he made one-piece, self-shank buttons for sale.

Wedgwood lived to see his jasper-ware buttons become so popular that potters everywhere were copying them. Despite many other inventions, Wedgwood's name became synonymous with jasper ware and despite the many hues and tints which he employed, his name became identified with the soft blue. His designs, which he commissioned from leading artists of the day, became classics.

Since their first great success, basaltes and jasper buttons, together with medallions for mounting, have had many fashion revivals. As with other Wedgwood pieces, it takes an experienced eye to distinguish early from late examples. A little-known Wedgwood type is shown in No. 9 on Plate 9. It is of glazed china decorated in polychrome and gold luster. The company, Josiah Wedgwood & Sons, Inc., dates it as 1925.

EIGHTEENTH-CENTURY BUTTONS

One of the periods in which buttons dominated costume began in Paris about 1775 and, as the interest spread to other capitals, lasted through the early decades of the nineteenth century. Pearl, passementerie, metal, and faced buttons, worn earlier in the century, became increasingly large, brilliant, and ornate. And as if these time-tested favorites could no longer satisfy the

48. *The making of a jasper-ware button.* (1.) Mold
for shaping the body. (2.) Mold for shaping ornament. (3.) Mold for shaping shank. (4.) Finished
button, back view. (5.) Same, front view. Courtesy
Josiah Wedgwood & Sons, Inc.

taste for spectacular display, a new type ap-
peared.

The fad started at Versailles where young men

49. (Above) *Buttons attributable to Wedgwood works.* Some with marks visible. (1-6.) Eighteenth century. (1.) French Revolution slogan, "Live Free or Die" on medallion, gilt mounting. (2.) Medallion set in silver with marcasites. (3.) Black with gold figure and wreath. (4.) Medallion set in polished steel mounting. (5.) Tricolor medallion set in gold. (6.) Medallion set in silver with paste. (7.) White body with sea-green or lilac center medallion. (8.) Tricolor medallion. (9.) Decorated luster with floral groupings and cobalt rim. Painted backmark, "Wedgwood," "22941M" Self-shank. (3, 7, 8.) Self-shanks with name "Wedgwood" impressed.

50. *A variety of pictures under glass.* (1.) Cut-outs (découpage) on opaque water-color (gouache) background. (2.) Painting on mica. (3.) Painting on pearl. (4.) Painting in gray on black (grisaille). (5.) Painting on the underside of glass with gold leaf (eglomise). (6.) Colored engraving. (7.) Cut-out and embossed paper over dark background (papyromania). (8.) Sculptured wax over metal foil. (9.) Featherwork.

placed pictures (often miniatures done by court painters), in metal button frames that were made like small shadow boxes with flat backs, deep sides, and glass tops. Plate 50. The numbers and kinds of pictures employed were unlimited. A fashion magazine of 1786 mentioned landscapes, cupids, and birds as the season's best subjects. A critic announced in 1787 that landscapes, flowers, cameos, insects, birds, symbolic subjects, hieroglyphics and monuments were all passé.

The eclipse proved brief, however. Even the destruction of the nobility, instead of discrediting extravagant buttons, made them more popular.

51. (Opposite) *Nineteenth-century enamels.* (1.) *Cloisonné.* Wires soldered to metal outline pattern and anchor enamel; much used in Orient. Front and back views. (2.) *Champlevé,* enamel anchored by partitions made directly in base, by stamping thin metal or gouging out thick. Type best suited to factory production. (3.) Encrusted. Drops of enamel, often backed by foil paillettes, made to simulate pearls, rubies, opals, and other gems. (4.) *Emaux peints* or enamel paints, in solution, used like water-color or oil paint for floral enamels, to tint transfer designs, and in Limoges portraits, as shown. (5.) *Plique-à-jour,* transparent enamel in suspension between filigree cells. When held to the light, resembles stained glass. Technique rare in buttons. (6.) *Basse-taille,* transparent enamel applied over decorative base, usually engine-turned metal or foil. Shown, a combination of turning and foil.

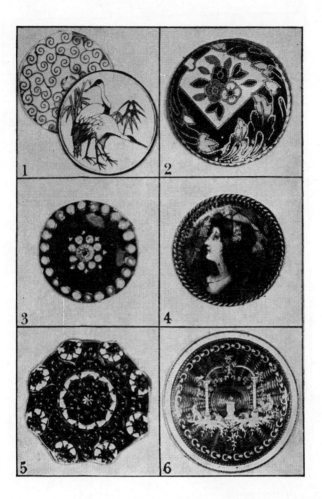

Popular as they were, underglass buttons were
by no means the only kind worn. A versatile and
inventive age used all the materials and techniques
at hand. Metal workers, gold- and silversmiths,

52. *Nineteenth-century buttons illustrating* emaux peints.

enamelers, potters, needleworkers, craftsmen in pearl, glass, ivory, lacquer, wood—all made buttons.

The buttons of the period might, in fact, be

taken as an index to the arts and crafts of the time without leaving any serious gaps. Probably no other epoch has ever produced beautiful buttons in so great a variety.

ENAMEL BUTTONS

The enamel palette holds all colors, transparent and opaque. Enamel, which is finely powdered glass, can be mixed to different consistencies and applied like a flux, handled like a paste, or brushed on like paint. Thus it has great artistic potentialities for those who master the technical proficiency required to process it.

Enamel buttons are made by fusing a coating of glass to a prepared base of gold, silver, copper, or brass. The surface of the base may be divided into segments separated by shallow partitions forming cells to hold the enamel in place. If the surface is smooth, the button must be enameled on the back as well as on the front to form a complete cover. After the enamel has been applied the button must be fired in a kiln under virtual laboratory conditions.

A well-made enamel button is free from defects on the front, with no bubbles, no crazing, no dull spots. In very old or very elaborate work, there is compensation for faults. Poor quality commercial work, of which there is considerable, has little merit.

Among the strangest shanks devised for buttons, catgut stands out. Plate 53, Nos. 1-6. Yet it was in common use from about 1710 to 1825. It was still current when uniform buttons emerged as a special type, and many military buttons of the late eighteenth and early nineteenth centuries have catgut shanks.

This is the way buttons with catgut shanks were made: a disklike mold of bone, wood, horn, or ivory was faced with a decorative top of metal, pearl, fabric, glass, or combination of materials. The parts were joined by crimping the front over the mold, when that was possible,

53. (Opposite) *Buttons with catgut, cord, or thread backs.* Nos 1-6 have bone or wood backs and catgut or cord shanks. (1.) Back views, two ways of lacing. (2.) Pierced pearl over colored foil, parts fastened together with band. (3.) Openwork metal over reverse-painted glass over foil. (4.) Thick faceted mirrored glass. Silver rim. (5.) Repoussé metal crimped over mold. French uniform button. (6.) Similar construction. The most usual types have metal faces. Nos. 6-12 are thread-backs from about 1850 to 1900. (7.) Back view, showing crisscrossed threads. (8.) Sepia transfer on ceramic medallion, parts fastened by metal rim. (9.) Lacquered paper glued to metal, bound by metal rim. (10.) Beaded cover, long-stitch back. (11.) Tole (painted metal). (12.) Repoussé metal, crimped over mold.

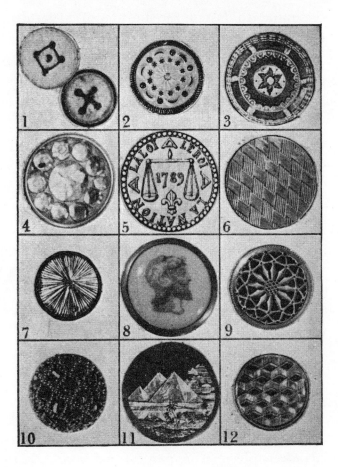

or by crimping a metal band around both parts. The shank, made before the front and back were joined, consisted of loops of catgut or strong cord laced through holes in the mold. Needle and thread were passed between the loops and the mold to fasten the button to a garment. Plate 53, No. 1 shows arrangement of catgut.

Long after such buttons had become curiosities, thread shanks were tried. Known as thread-backs, buttons with this shank were made by winding a mold, or a disk cut from cardboard or sheet metal, with a covering of stout thread. The fronts were put on, just as in the earlier day, by crimping or banding. Buttons with cloth-covered, crocheted, or beaded tops were given thread-backs by having the material drawn over the mold and fastened with long stitches back and forth to form a thick mat. From the front, these middle-to-late nineteenth-century buttons are indistinguishable from others with metal or canvas shanks.

INLAID BUTTONS

Inlaid buttons are made by embedding a design in a base. Base materials frequently used include papier mâché, natural and pressed horn, tortoise shell and imitations of it, ivory and imitations of it, celluloid, and a number of mixtures made in the nineteenth century by saturating a resinous substance with a pulpy filler. The inlays most frequently seen are of natural or dyed pearl, metal, horn, or ivory.

Without passing judgment on relative artistic

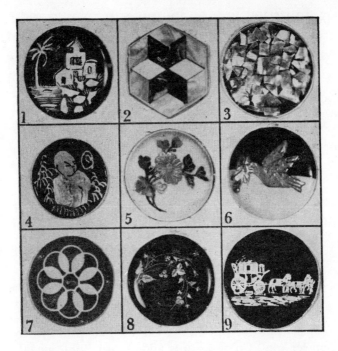

54. *Inlaid buttons.* Nos. 1-5 are pearl inlays. (1.) Horn. (2.) Veneered to bone. (3.) Tesserae in composition. (4.) Papier-mâché. (5.) Ivory. Nos. 6-9 have metal inlays. (6.) In celluloid. (7.) In composition. (8.) In tortoise shell. (9.) In rubber. (All are reduced in size except 6 and 7.)

merits, we can observe on Plate 54 that inlaying a button may be either a creative or a mechanical process. No. 5 is an ivory inlay for which the artist worked out the design, prepared the inlay, and carved the base. No. 8 was arranged on the tortoise shell and, when complete, incorporated

97

by subjection to heat and pressure. Nos. 7 and 9 are single-piece metal designs, preformed, and requiring only to be centered in the base. No. 3 is inlaid with pearl tesserae, which have only to be sprinkled in a button mold.

BONE, HORN, AND LEATHER BUTTONS

Long, long ago independent invention must have produced bone, horn, and leather buttons in many parts of the world. We know from

55. (Opposite) *Bone, horn, and leather.* (1.) Primitive bone button, from pre-historic times. (2.) Plain utility button, with nail-head shank, probably eighteenth century. (3.) Bone, carved like pearl, with power tool. Color accents added. (4.) Bone medallion, carved and pierced, set in metal frame, eighteenth century handwork. (5.) Stag horn, hand-carved. (6.) Natural bone, engraved and color rubbed in. (7.) Horn, reduced to a gelatinous mass, dyed and molded. Pattern is incised and gold-rubbed. (8.) Black plastic horn. Made of horn and hoof, softened and usually pulped. Portrait of Empress Eugénie. Many heads found in plastic horn. (9.) Back-mark of an English maker of a hundred years ago stamped in plastic horn. (10.) Plastic horn in a delicate all-over pattern. (11.) Upper, cross-section of true horn; lower, horn tip with metal mounting. (12.) Leather, tooled in the Florentine manner, mounted in a metal frame. (Nineteenth century, except as noted.)

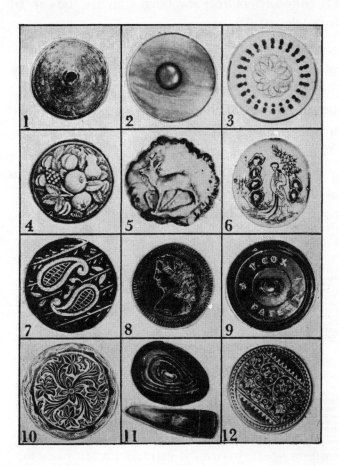

French records that bone was one of the very early modern button materials going back into the twelfth century.

It is well suited to practical wear by its light weight, sturdiness, and lack of abrasiveness. Aesthetically it equals ivory when expertly carved.

Osseous antlers, like staghorn, can also be carved into beautiful buttons.

Several entirely different kinds of buttons were made from true horn in the nineteenth century. Some were cut and polished to retain the qualities of natural horn. Some were dyed and molded under pressure until they looked like gelatin. The largest number were solid black, with a granular or stringy texture, pressed into patterns as sharp and clear as metal die-work. These buttons, known as plastic horn, were also made from hooves.

For some unknown reason leather buttons were not much worn during the last two centuries.

56. (Opposite) *Thread and fabric buttons in once-prevalent styles.* Nos. 1-3. Passementerie needlework of the eighteenth century. (4.) Embroidered cover, eighteenth century, (5.) Embroidered cover, nineteenth century. (6.) Hand-painted satin cover, nineteenth century. (7.) Dorset thread button, made with a needle over a flat mold and a tuft of cloth. (8.) Cloth especially woven for button covering. (9.) Fancy-shaped metal mold, machine-covered with three different fabrics. (10.) Crocheted with thread over a wooden mold. (11.) Silk cord worked over a bone mold. (12.) Machine eyelet-embroidery over colored silk.

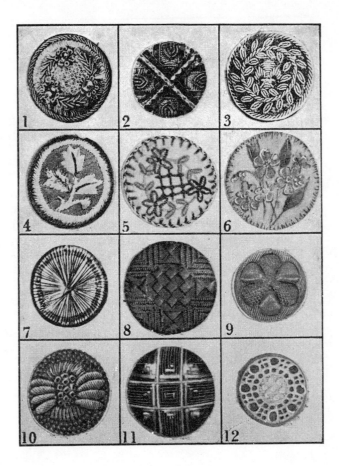

THREAD AND FABRIC BUTTONS

The idea of making buttons by covering rings, molds, and disks with a thread or cloth is very old. Machinery for fastening a smooth, tight

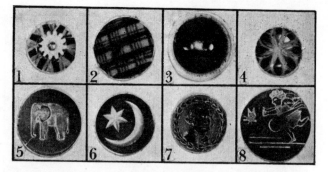

57. *Vegetable ivory buttons.* Late nineteenth or early twentieth century (1.) Carved with color accents and aluminum trim. (2-6.) Carved and dyed. (3.) Natural nut with bark as face ornamentation. (4.) Pierced and dyed. (5, 7, 8.) Embossed. (7.) A Stuart-like Washington head.

cover over a metal shell was perfected more than a hundred years ago. Inevitably the methods of making, the kinds of coverings, and the ways of decorating became as different as time and place could make them.

VEGETABLE-IVORY BUTTONS

For over a hundred years vegetable ivory buttons have been made from the inedible nuts of certain South American and African palms. Until plastics crowded them out, they were a major material. The nut is usually about the size and shape of a small egg; extra large ones yield buttons an inch and a quarter in diameter. A dark,

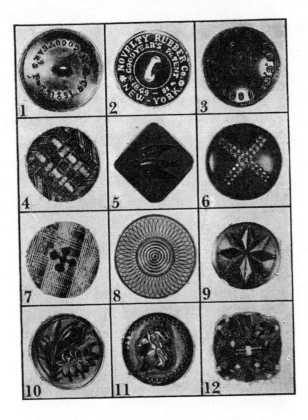

58. *Rubber buttons.* All Goodyear patents except
10 and 12. Nos. 1-4, 6-9, and 11 were made in several sizes; 10 and 12 are reduced in size.

rough bark covers a firm, cream-colored center,
grained like ivory. It is easy to work, can be
lightly embossed under pressure, and takes a
strong surface dye with no penetration.

Buttons with the name Goodyear and the date 1851 printed on the back are part of the history of the rubber industry. On May 6, 1851, Nelson Goodyear was granted a patent on his method of making rubber "hard and inflexible." He had seen Charles Goodyear fight against poverty and ridicule for twenty years, only to become embroiled in litigation over patents on vulcanization. No wonder Nelson wanted to protect his rights by documenting every button completely.

The backs of buttons made under his patent were half covered with printing: maker's name, patentee's name, and patent date in full. The marks make "Goodyear" an interesting specialty. Having been produced by only two factories and for only a few years, they form a closed series.

59. (Opposite) *Wooden buttons.* (1.) True primitive, devised by backwoodsmen from a notched piece of wood and a length of cord. Nos. 2-5. of Chinese workmanship. (2.) Carved teakwood. (3.) Intricately carved fruit pit set in metal frame. (4.) Turned ebony with ivory peg-shank. (5.) Cinnabar applied over a carved wood base in the early manner. (6. and 7.) Eighteenth-century buttons made on a lathe. (8. and 9.) Nineteenth-century lathe work. (10.) A trimming button carved from bogwood. (11.) A painted design of Hungarian origin. (12.) A sharp, clear-cut design obtained by stamping. (All are reduced in size.)

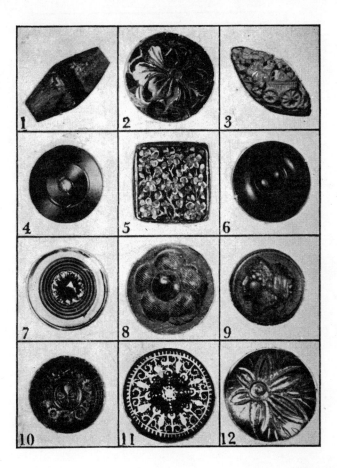

Over three hundred patterns in many sizes are known. Most of them are black; a few are brown, a few red. A *very* few are marked, "1849–1851."

Rubber buttons in fancy shapes and light colors, though later than Goodyears, are more scarce.

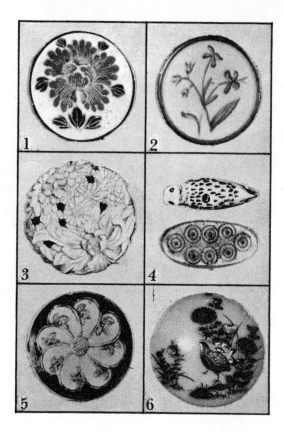

WOODEN BUTTONS

Collectors refer to small wooden. objects—carved, turned, inlaid, and pressed—as treen and give buttons a place in that field. Plate 59.

60. (Opposite) *Ivory buttons from three continents.* Nos. 1, 3 and 6 from the Orient. (1.) Painted and gilded. (3.) Carved in full relief with open work. (6.) Ivory base, inlaid with pearl, wood, horn, and wax, accented with engraving and pigment, an oriental blend of imagination and realism. Similar buttons made for China traders a hundred years ago. All these finely detailed. Nos. 2 and 5 of European origin. (2.) Painted. (5.) Carved. (4.) A toggle and a button made of walrus ivory in Alaska. The toggle is an indigenous type; both, authentic examples of native design and craftsmanship. (All reduced in size.)

IVORY BUTTONS

Ivory offers color and texture, beautiful with or without tinting, an ideal surface on which to paint or draw, and a structure well suited to carving and engraving. Though it is not an exacting material, it rewards the competent artist.

SPECIALTIES

Several button types, known as Specialties, have a place in the general collection. Cuff buttons, lapel buttons, and studs are in this category. (Plate 62.) Bridle buttons, well remembered by the older generation as colorful harness fastenings which held the bridle reins, netsukes from Japan, and mandarin buttons from China are also classed as Specialties.

The netsuke (pronounced ne-tske in Japanese)

61. *Netsukes, the native Japanese button.* Various sizes.

Plate 61 *(above)* is a costume accessory found nowhere else in the world and now almost obsolete in Japan, as Western clothes have replaced the kimono. Traditionally, Japanese men prized the netsuke so much for personal adornment that netsuke carvers became artists of the highest ability and netsuke carving was recognized as one of the fine arts.

The netsuke is an ingenious, small object, made of wood, ivory, coral, or any material suitable for carving. The subjects are as varied as the clever Japanese mind can devise. In the base of the netsuke are two connecting holes, which are strung with a drawstring when the button is worn. The purpose of a netsuke is to anchor the string which fastens a tobacco pouch, purse, or other personal necessity to the kimono sash. In one of its button-like uses the netsuke holds the drawstring tight around a pocket, formed from a gathering of the sash fabric.

As Europeans and Americans have been buying netsukes ever since the first traders discovered them, many fine ones have gone into collections. The demand for them became so great that for a long time they have been made purely for export.

Mandarin buttons, on the other hand, were never an export from China, and those in the West were brought back by travelers. They were worn only by men of wealth and position. Their colors signified the nine ranks of civil and military position, which before 1912 existed in China under the Manchus.

62. *Cuff buttons.* Nos. 1-6. (1.) Enameled. (2.) Damascene. (3.) Moss agate set in gold. (4.) Metal device on pearl. (5.) White metal. (6.) Crystal intaglio design. *Studs,* Nos. 7-9. (7. and 9.) Metal inlays in horn. Reduced in size. (8.) Photograph of Queen Victoria, with chased aluminum rim.

The button, composed of a bead (about the size of a crab apple), was mounted upright on a metal standard. This could be unscrewed and fastened to the top of a mandarin hat. It stood about two inches high, and to us looks more like a hatpin than a button.

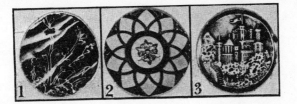

63. *Celluloid buttons.* (1.) Grained body with pressed design. (2.) Colored body under pierced metal top. (3.) Ivoroid.

CELLULOID BUTTONS

Celluloid, the first synthetic plastic widely used for buttons, can be processed to imitate many materials, among them glass, paper, tortoise shell, and ivory. It can also be made up with new characteristics of color and texture. Ordinary celluloid in opaque sheets was used like cloth to cover buttons. In transparent sheets, it was mounted over foil to give luminous effects. Celluloid can be colored, grained, and embossed to look like carved ivory. Called ivoroids, such buttons are considered choice by collectors.

PLASTICS

The late 1930s brought great changes to the button world when manufacturers of synthetic plastics began supplying button-makers with raw material. In a field where previously no plastic except celluloid had been successfully used, a

64. *Modern plastic buttons.* Reduced in size, except No. 12, which is enlarged.

new age came almost overnight. Strange technical terms—polystrene, acetate, urea, and butrate—were added to the button lexicon with new trade names like Catalin, Plaskon, and Lucite.

The quick public acceptance of these entirely new materials, the revolutionary methods of fabrication, and the chameleon qualities they possessed stimulated both technicians and artists. It seemed as though anything that could be dreamed up could be successfully made. The designer did not even have to worry about such a problem as the weight of a button, for plastics were so light that bulk was no obstacle.

In some quarters, fancy buttons were entirely cut loose from traditional designs and given startlingly novel, not to say bizarre appearances. One season featured knots and bows of plastic strands; another ran to spaghetti-like twists.

Amusing novelty buttons caught the collector's eye and were nicknamed "goofies." Goofies are buttons realistically shaped like objects. They hit the market about 1938 and have never completely disappeared since. Buttons in the shapes of nuts, fruits, vegetables, flowers, animals, persons, toys, articles of clothing—all kinds of objects—were carded and sold in sets of identical buttons, sets of assorted colors, and sets of assorted objects. The buttons were amusing and low-priced, selling for a penny or two each in the thirties. The search it takes now to find certain rare goofies needed to complete a set illustrates again how rapidly things can disappear.

Although novelty plastics, goofies, and others,

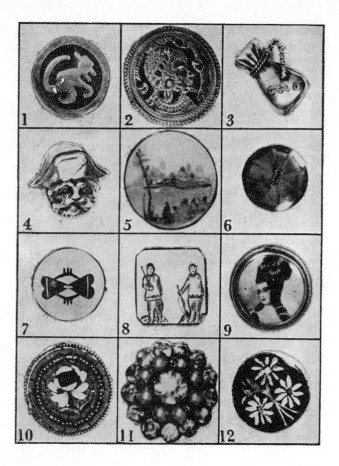

65. (Opposite) *Modern buttons from seven regions.* (1. 2.) Central America, silver. (3.) United States, silver. (4.) France, metal. (5.) South America, vegetable ivory. (6.) Denmark, amber. (7.) United States, Zia Indian pottery. (8.) Aleutian Islands, ivory. (9.) Italy, lithograph. (10.) Italy, glass mosaic. (11.) Czechoslavakia, pearls and paste jewels. (12.) Mexico, painted wood. Various sizes.

are popular, attention is not limited to them. Paperweights, in which flowers or other articles are encased in clear plastics, are favorites, as are crystal plastics, carved and colored in reverse, and many other lovely kinds.

On Plate 64 Nos. 1-3, Lucite paperweights; 4, 6, 7, 9. Goofies; 5, 10. Pictorial; 8, 11, 12, Novelties.

MODERN STUDIO BUTTONS

As collectors brought old buttons to public attention by exhibiting their finest examples, we heard echoes of interest in the craft studios where creative artisans were at work. Seeing what had been done in the past and finding an eager clientele for similar work, artists were inspired to try their skill at making buttons from glass, enamel, ceramics, metal, stone, or other materials. (Plate 66.)

Since paperweights were so much admired by button collectors, glassmakers began working over their lamps. In a short time, several men were making buttons of marvelous beauty, comparable to the best from the past, without being imitations. Much of the new work in enamel, metal and ceramics copies old patterns, some of it follows the strong line of modern jewelry of flowing form.

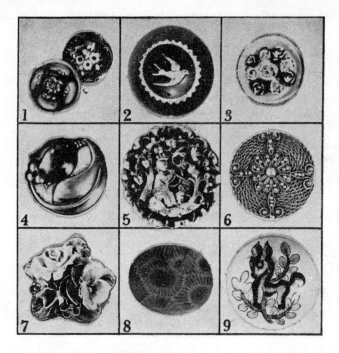

66. *Modern buttons made for collectors by studio artists.* Nos. 1-3. "Paperweights." Actual size. Nos. 4-6. Metal work in gold and silver. Reduced in size. Nos. 7-9. Ceramic, native stone, and enamel. Reduced in size.

The lapidary contributes by taking what appears to be an ordinary stone and cutting and polishing it into a semiprecious gem.

Studio work done as a handicraft is significant. It applies the best contemporary talent to the old medium of buttons and offers new categories to the modern collector.

The button department in a large store today looks much like the jewelry section. Buttons, artistically arranged and skillfully lighted, are kept in glass cases. Stock is presented on sample cards brought out as required. It is hardly necessary to remark that buttons are now high style and that never before in this century have they been so important as costume accessories.

The fashion is strongly toward what we might call neo-Victorian pieces, with an occasional reversion to much earlier times. The making of black and luster glass has been resumed exactly as it was fifty years ago. Makers of fine paste have copied antique mountings. Owners of the pictorial dies used for stamping metal buttons have put them to use again. Italian mosaics are being mounted, also ceramic plaques. Coin buttons have returned. All materials, even plastics, are given an antique look.

This modern revival has brought buttons into focus as objects of considerable tradition. Plate 65.

III. BUTTONS ON DISPLAY

Newspaper stories about button shows and special exhibits attract wide attention, bringing thousands of readers to a better appreciation of the hobby. Radio and television interviews emphasize the news value of such events. Few people, however, realize what opportunities there are for seeing fine buttons on permanent display in museums and elsewhere. In New York City alone, a collector could spend weeks over the collections in museums.

COOPER UNION MUSEUM

At the Cooper Union Museum for the Arts of Decoration you can see a well-classified and arranged collection, rich in eighteenth-century pearls, steels, bone-backs, passementeries, and pictorial buttons. The museum library, one of the world's best on costume, provides a wealth of background and auxiliary material on the subject of buttons.

The Traphagen School of Fashion has some extraordinarily fine costumes with the original buttons (Plate 5), and also an attractively displayed collection, mostly of nineteenth-century costume buttons.

B. BLUMENTHAL & COMPANY, NEW YORK

In the showrooms of the importing firm, B. Blumenthal & Company, hangs a magnificent exhibit of pearl buttons which won an award at the Exposition Universelle in Paris in 1878. Only mother-of-pearl of the finest quality was used for buttons, which were made to reveal the skills of the craftsman. The smallest ones, for gloves and infant's dresses, are no larger than the head of a common pin. Those with pictorial carving are true cameos and a few measure two inches in diameter.

BAILEY, GREEN & ELGER, INC., NEW YORK

Bailey, Green & Elger, Inc., manufacturers and importers, have in their showrooms the exhibit of pearl buttons that won a Gold Medal at the Philadelphia Centennial in 1876. There you can also see a massive wall cabinet and twelve movable frames, which house an exhibit set up more than fifty years ago by a French button maker to preserve the entries on which he had won awards at important expositions in France and elsewhere between 1849 and 1900.

Both of these importing companies sponsor traveling exhibits of antique as well as modern buttons. These can be seen from time to time in leading department stores.

METROPOLITAN MUSEUM OF ART

The Costume Institute of the Metropolitan Museum has rich resources in costume buttons. Its study materials were increased many fold by the recent gift of the Hanna Sicher Kohn Memorial Collection. The Kohn Collection is comprehensive, containing excellent examples from the entire field. It is exceptionally strong in eighteenth-century sets, sporting and hunt-club buttons, exotic materials, unusual craftsmanship, and unique items of importance.

The Institute, in addition to this collection, owns many original buttons found on some of the seven thousand articles of dress in its files. It also has a large library of prints and books on costume.

NEW-YORK HISTORICAL SOCIETY

The student of military buttons will find a visit to the New-York Historical Society rewarding. A half-century of research has gone into this large and magnificent collection that was assembled through the systematic exploration of camp sites of the Revolution and the War of 1812.

FORT TICONDEROGA MUSEUM

In upstate New York, the Fort Ticonderoga Museum has military buttons displayed in such a way that they interest both student and casual visitor. The cases hold buttons worn by the three armies, French, British, and American, which fought around the battlements in colonial times. Excavations on the site have yielded rare specimens of unquestionable authenticity. The buttons are carefully arranged and well labeled. Realistic wax figures in original eighteenth-century uniforms display buttons in actual use.

ESSEX INSTITUTE OF SALEM

The Essex Institute of Salem, Massachusetts, has published a catalogue of the Emilio Collection which it received as a gift in 1910. You can see there especially the buttons worn by early American, Confederate, and British regiments which fought in America. The Messerve

Collection of dress buttons is also on view at the Institute.

For sheer numbers, visit the Connecticut State Museum in Hartford. You will find *more* buttons there than in any of the places we have mentioned. There are 90,000 of them, and this is how they came to be assembled. In 1883 a business man, John H. Tingue, offered a prize of fifty dollars to each young lady who would send him a string of 2500 buttons, all with shanks, and no two alike (a Charm String plus, as it were). The press took up the story and the next thing Mr. Tingue knew he had spent $4,000 and acquired 90,000 buttons. Soon after he gave them to the Agricultural Society of Connecticut, which showed no great appreciation of the gift until recently. After years of neglect, the Tingue collection has been brought out of its dark cases and rearranged into smaller displays, for the museum does not have adequate room to show all of it all of the time.

JUST BUTTONS MUSEUM

The Sally Lewis House at Southington, Connecticut, contains the Just Buttons Museum which has changing exhibits and a program of activities.

THE B. GRACE PORTER MEMORIAL COLLECTION

The best-known exhibit in the Middle West is in Springfield, Ohio, where the local chapter of the Daughters of the American Revolution has a button room in its museum headquarters. This collection came through the bequest of Miss B. Grace Porter, who spent years bringing it together.

THE LIGHTNER MUSEUM

In the South you should visit the Lightner Museum at St. Augustine, Florida. The uniform buttons there, built up around the famous Reginald Hart Collection, include many fine items. The large section of costume buttons was started by Mr. Lightner and later developed as a memorial to Marguerite Maple, pioneer collector and co-author of *Button Classics*.

OTHER OPPORTUNITIES TO SEE BUTTONS

The museums mentioned are double-starred by the well-traveled button hobbyist. The observant traveler has also learned to look further for buttons, finding them not only where they are conspicuously displayed, but where they are half hidden. He explores places like Memorial Hall in Philadelphia, the Confederate Museum at Richmond, Virginia, and Greenfield Village, at Dearborn, Michigan.

He searches wherever there are relics or restorations of pioneer life; he looks down the byways of science, invention, and industry; he notes what archaeologists put on display. Where there is carved ivory, he finds netsukes; in Wedgwood displays he sees medallions and buttons; among Indian arts and crafts, he locates Navaho silver buttons. And always he pays attention to the buttons on costumes, whether he is looking at an actual garment or a painting of one.

Among the special events, which are always well publicized, the most important is the annual show put on by the National Button Society. It has been held somewhere in the Middle West every fall since 1939. At present it draws almost 1500 competitive entries, each one a 9- by 12-inch frame of buttons. It also hangs a large noncompetitive section and an impressive number of educational exhibits loaned by museums and trade sources, as well as by members. The leading button dealers of the country take booths and offer buttons for sale. Forums, lectures, and demonstrations round out the show.

Many regional, state, and local shows are held regularly. Most antique shows and many hobby shows now include buttons as one of the features.

If you live in a community where there seem to be no buttons, no shows, no window displays, no newspaper or radio stories, no club programs on buttons, it is still probable that there is a collector in the vicinity who enjoys discussing his hobby with visitors. The membership list of the National Button Society may provide you with the name; if not, a little inquiry will, for when you begin talking about buttons you inevitably find other enthusiasts near at hand. Address the Society through the Secretary, 47 Keith Street, Springfield 8, Massachusetts.

BUTTON TERMS TO KNOW

Backmark. Any picture, symbol, word, number, or combination of these put on a button-back by the maker or decorator. Plates 24, 25, 32, 44, 47, 49.

Basse-taille. From the French, meaning bas-relief; applied to a kind of transparent enamel work with sculptured background. Plate 51, No. 6.

Bull's-mouth. A shell with a dark red underlayer.

Cabochon. A gem or imitation stone, shaped in convex form, polished but not faceted.

Calico. Applied to buttons in patterns copied from calico cloth. Plate 46, Nos. 1-6.

Card, original. A card of buttons prepared for selling to a retail costumer.

Card, sample. A card prepared for a display or for a salesman with a full line of sizes and colors, one button of each kind.

Ceramics. All buttons made of baked clay, such as earthenware, pottery, semiporcelain and porcelain.

Class. The category according to which buttons

are brought together on the basis of material, period, construction, design or other features which all members of a class have in common. The classifications of the National Button Society include hundreds of classes which help collectors to find meaningful groupings. See Plate 18 as an example, *Heads of Famous People.*

Cloisonné. A technique for enameling in which the enamel is held in place by cells formed by soldering wires to a solid base. Plate 51, No. 1.

Conversion. A false button which has been produced by fastening a button-shank to some other object, such as the top of a hatpin, or by mounting some other object, such as a medal, in a button frame.

Cowrie. A brown and white mottled shell with a lavender underlayer.

Damascening. A method of decorating metal by undercutting the surface with fine lines and hammering metal thread of contrasting color into the grooves. Used chiefly by Oriental button-makers. Plate 7. No. 7.

Dapt. To shape a flat button plate convexly.

Decalcomania. The process of decorating buttons by transferring pictures or designs from specially prepared papers to the plain surfaces.

Emaux peints. Translated from the French, as painted enamels. Plate 52.

Fortification agate. An agate having angular markings suggesting the plan of a fortification. Plate 43, No. 10.

Frame, Houghton. The frame generally used for buttons mounted in the standard way. It is a glass-topped, box-type, hanging frame made of wood, constructed so that cards can be easily slipped in and out. D. D. Houghton, of Orrville, Ohio, is the designer and manufacturer.

Goldstone. (Also called aventurine.) An opaque glass saturated with copper particles which sparkle and appear golden. Plate 40, No. 11.

Hallmark. The official mark required by British law on all objects of gold and silver, and, by extension, similar marks used on precious metals in other countries. The British marks are stamped in code and when interpreted give the maker's name, the town and year of manufacture, and for some periods show that the tax has been paid. Plate 23, No. 8.

Incroyable and merveilleuse. From the French meaning "incredible gentleman and amazing lady." The term applied to a popular button subject picturing couples dressed in the extreme fashions of the French Directoire. Also called Fops. See Plate 52, No. 12.

Latticino. A lacy pattern made of milk-white

canes or threads of white glass. Plate 38, No. 19.

Line. The unit of measurement used in the button trade and by some collectors. Forty lines equal one inch.

Lithograph. A reproduction made by surface printing from a drawing made on a special base with a special ink. Plate 20, Nos. 4-6, 8.

Mounting, standard. (See also *Size* below.) An arrangement of buttons according to the rules for competition in shows of the National Button Society. Requirements are that 9 by 12-inch cards be used and that the number of buttons mounted be governed by their size:

Large buttons, twenty to a card.

Medium-sized, thirty to a card.

Small-sized, forty-two to a card.

Diminutives, seventy to a card.

Various sizes, twenty-five to a card.

Mounting patterns. Designs for the attractive arrangement of the requisite number of buttons on a card. See Plate 67 for suggestions.

Nacreous. Iridescent, as in the pearly inner layer of various shells.

Niello. A method of decorating gold or silver buttons (or other objects), by applying a special metal alloy to an etched design and firing it. The finished piece has the appearance of a

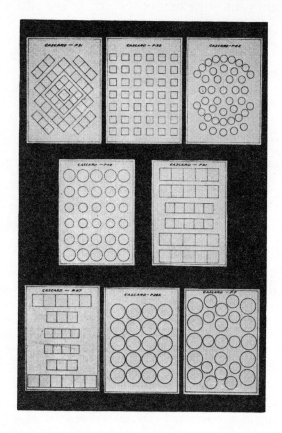

67. *Mounting patterns.* Courtesy, The Cassidys, Makers of "Cascards," Wellington, Ohio.

design drawn in black upon gold, or when used on silver, a niello design appears to be heavily oxidized. Plate 23, No. 9.

Paillette. A spangle.